ALSO BY C.D. WRIGHT

ShallCross

*The Poet, the Lion, Talking Pictures, El Farolito, a Wedding in St. Roch,
the Big Box Store, the Warp in the Mirror, Spring, Midnights, Fire & All*

One With Others [a little book of her days]

Rising, Falling, Hovering

One Big Self: An Investigation

Like Something Flying Backwards: New and Selected Poems (UK)

Cooling Time: An American Poetry Vigil

One Big Self: Prisoners of Louisiana, photographs by Deborah Luster, with
text by C.D. Wright

Steal Away: Selected and New Poems

Deepstep Come Shining

Tremble

The Lost Roads Project: A Walk-In Book of Arkansas,
with photographs by Deborah Luster

Just Whistle: a valentine,
with photographs by Deborah Luster

String Light

Further Adventures with You

Translations of the Gospel Back into Tongues

C.D. Wright

Casting Deep Shade

AN AMBLE INSCRIBED TO BEECH TREES & CO.

WITH PHOTOGRAPHS BY DENNY MOERS

COPPER CANYON PRESS
PORT TOWNSEND, WASHINGTON

for WILLIAM S. MERWIN *and* PAULA S. MERWIN

THE BEECH HAS TO DO WITH THRESHOLDS

BEN LERNER

This is a book about a genus of trees (beech). And their foliate language ("The hanger-on-until-spring leaf is *marcescent*"). And arboreal lore ("Beech in the house interferes with a spirit's passing"). And the root systems of the beech in poetry (although Virgil, the poet suggests, might have confused the beech and chestnut). It is a book about the material of books ("Beech is Anglo-Saxon *bóc:* book, document, or charter"), the origins of art in nature. It is also a book, how could it not be, about climate: "It's all about global warming, baby." It is also, how could it not be, about property, as the poet pokes around the grounds of mansions in search of rare specimens or elegizes copses razed in the name of development. It is a book full of love and admiration for eccentric arborists and purveyors of folk knowledge, for they are—like the poet—committed to keeping the language and landscape particular, unpredictable, collective. Committed to preserving these slow-growth kinetic sculptures under siege by profiteers and voles. This is an *un*-commonplace book. And this is a book of vivid childhood memories tethered to trees of various sorts:

> For Christmas we were committed to the red cedar. Dad would drive down a random dirt road or two-lane highway until he spied a loner outside a fence line. Or just inside (easy to jump the fence if a bull came charging). He thought it was stupid to buy a tree, and viewed them as common property. One year I nagged him into flocking the tree, and I readily call up the slap-stick sight of him pinning the top of the tree to the clothesline and spraying phony snow from an aerosol canister in a big wind, cussing like the country soul he was, while he flocked himself and the hapless cedar for the first and last time. Then the poor freakish-looking thing was mounted at a tilt in a minnow bucket full of rocks with Mother's unfinished felt tree skirt bunched up around it. Once both my brother and I had left home, the parents settled on an aluminum tree Mother left up year-round adorned with uniform ice-blue balls.

Even a description of holiday kitsch can—through the specificity of her language and the action of her syntax—yield a little lyric miracle in the hands of this poet. Who grew outside the fence lines of any school or style. If you don't yet know her writing, this is a fine place for a first encounter, here among the beeches. Then you can follow the bewitching voice back through the dozen other volumes. If, like me, you have long depended on her body of work, perhaps you will also be grateful for this book's lack of finality. A work in a perpetual state of becoming. A provisionality acknowledged in the printing: the text bound to the center block is more embraced by the wraparound cover than contained. I for one would rather have this live graph of her process than any species of closure. The pages just hanging on. At the threshold.

She was a loner only in the sense that she sounded like no one else, adhered to no fad or orthodoxy, but she worked frequently with artists and friends, was "one with others." ("The beech is gregarious, says one. / The beech prefereth its own company, says another.") It is fitting that this project is in part a collaboration with the photographer Denny Moers, who captured the images that appear on many of her covers. For this is also a book about looking—as was the great *Deepstep Come Shining,* which the present title shadows. Moers's "watersmoothsilversatin" photographs (as the poet describes beech bark, almost quoting e.e. cummings) complement her sustained acts of attention, the slow exposure of her gaze, as she takes in a tree and its ramifications. Other images tipped in by her longtime editor Michael Wiegers make this amble both a family album and a work of poetic taxonomy. It is both C.D.'s book and a loving tribute to her. To her strength and receptivity. "Beech bark is a tender thing."

We seldom appreciate any possession during its abundance, nor until it has disappeared is its want felt.

JOHN PINKNEY BROWN, *Practical Arboriculture*

A beech is, in almost any landscape where it appears,
the finest tree to be seen.

DONALD CULROSS PEATTIE, *A Natural History of North American Trees*

The Copper or Purple-leaf Beech, of which the best form is always a grafted tree, Rivers' Purple or 'Riversii', is an upsetting sight in our green landscape, and can set at nought the most carefully conceived schemes when seen at a distance. It should occasionally be planted within the ambit of a dwelling, but not too near. The Cut-leaf or Fern-leaf Beech, *F.s.* 'Heterophylla' or 'Asplenifolia', makes a fine compact specimen tree, standing singly, but has no value in the landscape.

GRAHAM STUART THOMAS, *Trees in the Landscape*

Casting Deep Shade

Poses no significant litter problem.

Ranks as "not particularly outstanding" according to the Forest Service.

Stone Age men dined on beechnuts with their clubby hirsute hands.

Iron Age man made beechnut flour.

Native Americans made beechnut flour.

Most runes were carved in yew but beech was an acceptable substitute.

A recipe for beechnut butter is easy to obtain.

A lot of nutrients in the fruit of chestnut, oak, beech. Same mealy, meaty family.

Can hold a nail but tends to split when nailed.

Can hold a curve.

As in, the turned parts of the "democratic" Windsor chair.

Except when green.

Nut is rich in oil, of pleasant flavor.

The Druids grew wise eating their nuts.

The pollen record keeps going back and back.

Pollen from pre-Roman peats has been found in the UK.

In a dream it signifies wisdom, else, death.

Is brittle.

In aromatherapy, a confidence booster.

Windfirm if the soil is not shallow.

Limbs low.

Beech, *Fagus*. Family Fagaceae. Alternating leaves of the *sylvatica* (European) crenated, of the *grandifolia* (American) crenulated; the former a little wavy, the latter a little toothy. Deciduous, monoecious, smooth, silver-grey bark, fruits three-angle nuts, in a bristly involucre, averaging 80 feet, can live 500 years, though standard is 200–300.

American beech (*Fagus grandifolia*) is not the priority here, only because it is rarely among the beeches I see daily where I live in southern New England. Their masses having been greatly diminished since settlers grasped that they grew in soil good for farming.

At the upper end of the Appalachian Trail in the Adirondacks, long after the settlers cleared the land and killed off enough timber wolf and cougar, deer populations began to snowball. Logging took much birch and maple, beech becoming dominant. By the 1960s, beech bark disease (BBD) took out 9 of 10 trees in massive chunks of forest, with the new shoots carrying the same doomed DNA.

The disease has moved into lower elevations. A student at the University of Tennessee studied clonality in the beech gaps in 2006. She found zero resistance to BBD. *Zero.*

In the early nineties, the Adirondacks were beech-death country.

Where beech bark disease has struck, smaller, weaker, or soon-to-be-infected offspring follow.

Ghost trees are those dying of beech bark. They turn white.
(I personally have never seen a ghost.)

Along the southern Appalachian forest trail there are more tree species than any other forest in North America.

In the Pleistocene, beech spanned the continent.

Stands and groves and mixed woods are still not so rare.

The European or common beech (*Fagus sylvatica*) is, however, at hand, here specifically being Rhode Island, though it has never, as the keeper of the Arnold Arboretum in Boston, MA, told me, been known to go rogue.

Would that it would.

Escapes, it is written, are to be expected.

Europeans run low on self-fertility, at least on this continent.

In skin cosmetology, the tree holds the curious designation of vegetal placenta.

Powder from the beech in the right shoe will show you to your fortune.

Individual specimens, allées, and hedges of the European cultivars are strikingly present in the East, especially in New England. Rhode Island is the hub for the European beech, foremost, the copper beech.

American beech has 15 pairs of leaf veins as opposed to 5–9 or 10 on Europeans.

You've got your lamina, midribs, veins on the top of the leaf; the lenticels on the main stem, the petiole (the leaf stem), the axil with axillary bud. The leaf is where it's at: water from the soil, CO_2 from the air: photosynthesis *et voilà,* sugar and O_2. Storing sugar keeps the tree going through winter, flowering in spring, and making leaves.

The *Manual of Woody Plants* lists 43 cultivars of the *Fagus sylvatica,* though only a handful are commonly grafted.

Of the European or common beech preferred varieties are: purple, weeping, copper, and fern leaf.

The Europeans sometimes call it the Queen Beech.
Though they well know he/she is AC/DC.

In his 19th-century *Portraits of Forest Trees,* Jacob George Strutt insisted "they give added beauty
and variety to an abode fitly chosen for the favoured residence of royalty."

The word *copse* was used to describe trees that sheltered game. Also, *holt.*
Both winsome words: cool-down, darkling, and tranquilizing.

A *grove* is meant to be a small collection without undergrowth.

A *coppice* emerges from cut trees, the new shoots that spring
from the stool that are then cut again for fuel and lumber.

Shoots grow faster in the dark.

The 70 acres of Blithewold Arboretum in Bristol, RI, were intended to be a horticultural
wonder, and the superintendent of Prospect Park in Brooklyn, a Bristol native, was hired to
plan the grounds. The mansion on the land was a part-time home for Augustus Van Wickle,
a coal baron's son, and his wife, Bessie, a coal baron's daughter. Augustus lost his life shooting
skeet. Shooting himself by mistake.

Nearby Mount Hope Farm, the 1745 estate of Rhode Island's first governor, William Bradford, is now a country inn for weddings and other celebrations, recently adding on an annual 5K footrace. There you will find our early exemplars of *F. sylvatica.* Gov. Bradford was elected to the Continental Congress of 1776, and didn't go (an abrupt and jabbing reminder that I held a free ticket to the Concert for Bangladesh and didn't go. I sat in my sublet in Greenwich Village like a self-satisfied house cat and did not go).

A pollard is a tree cut at the top and at upper branches to stimulate new growth. There are covetable, pollarded apples at Blithewold Arboretum. Sweet for the picking in low heels.

Once pollarded, keep pollarding.

There are pollarded nonblooming mulberries in front of San Francisco's City Hall that disturb my pathways. No surprise that they were used in the ending of *Invasion of the Body Snatchers* (1978). I have lately been informed they are London plane hybrid sycamores. Evidently shipped from Japan. For the World's Fair. After the big quake of 1906.

Withies, also referred to as osiers, come from pollarded crack willows.

Withies are not in big demand, but cricket bats are yet made from crack willow.

Withies and osiers, not much to do with beeches. Nor are switch willows much in demand for the back side of bare legs instead of a fired-up hand or belt-spanking at which point I was wearisomely hard to catch.

~

The dawn redwoods on our block in Rhode Island tower over a neighbor's 20-year-old neocolonial house and the immaculate, uneventful lawn the twins occupy. I am both glad and sad that they are here. They make the house look fictitious. They demand so much more water than I imagine they can draw here. Classified as critically endangered. Yet they appear healthy. A volunteer can be glimpsed in the back corner of their lot. Ready to step in when the elders cross over.

There is a small stand of *Fagus grandifolia* in Arnold Arboretum in Boston, and I visited a cluster in Lost Valley in the Arkansas Ozarks when I was there in May for some literary confab. I mentioned beeches to a woman in Little Rock and the next morning she came back with an e-mail of detailed directions from one whom I would call an extreme nurseryman from the Arkansas Delta, repatriated in Carroll County (where my father was born; which we were encouraged to call the Holy Land).

The annual pilgrimage to the Judge's homestead was mandatory. The thorn trees, thistle, and colossal cow pies made the ramble almost impassable. The log house had burned donkey's years before, replaced by a one-room clapboard, now up to the rafters with then-owner Raymond Fletcher's uncategorizable stuff. Grandma Wright's peonies still bloomed. She must have set them when she was a young bride with a shabby trunk of bleached flour sacks for a trousseau. The end sheet of Grandma Wright's Bible includes the following family record, in its entirety, in her jiggly hand:

Harley Wright
oprated on April 23, 1966

Ernie Wright
and
Aline Collins
was married Friday
Aug 22, 1941

Noah that
Built the ark
was 950 years old
when he died
Hot water heater was
put in Jan 18, 1954

Raymond Fletcher, Dad's childhood friend, was an Ozark hoarder, way before it was a diagnosis. He asked Dad to help him make out a holographic will, but having been forced out of his own house by his glut of reserves, he had moved into a trailer in which he alone could gain access to the clear side of the bed, and since the cab of his truck would barely accommodate him, he and my father sat on the tailgate and made up the will. The rest of us stood upwind of the gentle, smelly fellow.

The red, hand-lettered sign on a mailbox before reaching Fletcher's boundary line read Strine's Poor Farm. Fletcher owned about 1,200 acres: pasture, creek, trees, cows; bulging junked school buses, trucks on blocks, loaders, outbuildings, his own farmhouse, Dad's childhood farmhouse, barns, rotten sheds, all choking on things no one could inventory without surrendering their life to the cause. Beeches are far too fastidious for that environment.

(Dad resisted the temptation to buy the old property, fortunately, as he had the exact same Great Depression–induced waste-not-want-not disposition that living inside the city limits had restricted to his basement, a terrifying realm. For the most part, the surplus was confined to discount vitamins and medical publications for the lay. Dad wanted to live a long and fruitful life. He did.)

In olden times, Dad and Raymond Fletcher rigged up crank phones between the family houses. (Worked real well.)

American beeches can/do thrive in the East. Yet northwest Arkansas is still in their range; quite a few can/do cross the big brown river. They prefer their own company, but they are still a minority of the mix of temperate broadleaf forests.

The largest trees are usually found in the Ohio and Mississippi River Valleys where they can live to be 300–400 years old.

The rivers meet at Cairo ("kay-roe"), IL, in that Southerly part of the North known as Little Egypt.

The owner of Ridgecrest Gardens, lately of Carroll County, AR, wrote: *The beech trees are rather clannish… and disdainful of civilization or disturbance, keeping to themselves primarily in remote hollows in pristine areas that have not recently been timbered or grazed or frequently burned. They are at their best expression in Arkansas on the southern half of Crowley's Ridge, and in the Buffalo watershed.*

Crowley's Ridge is coated with a windblown sediment known as loess or rock flour. That's where your kitty litter comes from. Grasses keep it from flying all over. Beeches don't mind loess. Nor do peach trees, judging from the sweet Elbertas that grew there—where Hemingway penned *A Farewell to Arms* when he was married to Pauline. It is the only rise in the Alluvial Plain of Old Man River. In the event the river floods, rather, *when,* head for the Ridge.

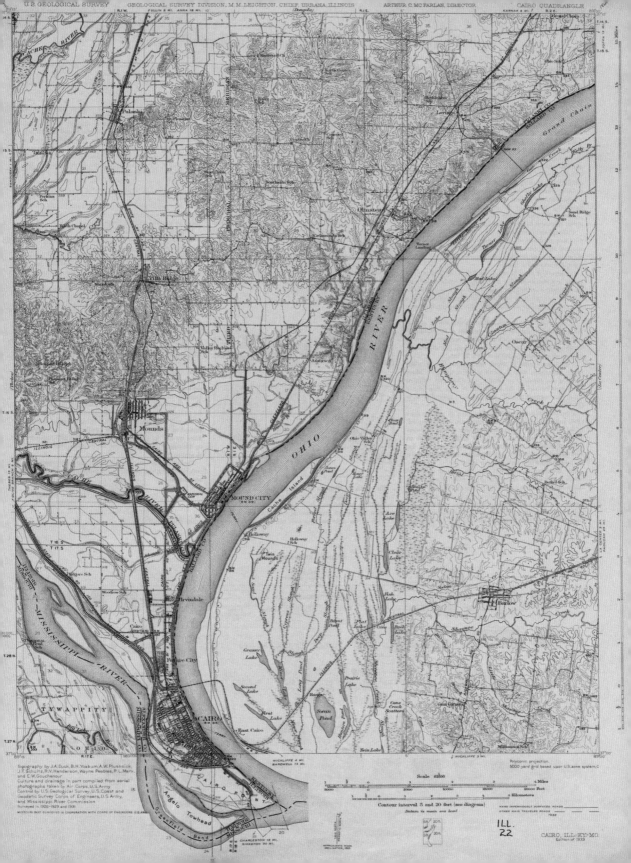

Elbertas, old-fashioned freestones of the tart variety, have been phasing out since post-WWII. Then the feds eliminated tariffs on imports. Sales to Trader Joe's and Whole Foods disappeared 10 years ago. And that's all Elberta wrote.

Nearest town to Crowley's Ridge is Paragould, birthplace of Iris DeMent, the 14th youngun, who left there for Los Angeles at three. Make no mistake, she's a downhome Delta songbird. I believe her singing, Pentecostal family came from one of those no-name, numbered islands in the big river.

Says Larry Lowman:

…Taking a detour east from 21 in Boxley Valley to go toward Ponca will take you to the access road for Lost Valley hiking trail. This would be where I would take someone to see beeches close at hand.… The trail is easy…and you begin to see beeches almost immediately. The ice storm of 2009 devastated many of the elders in the beech tribe here, but several fine individuals remain and some good youthful ones survived.

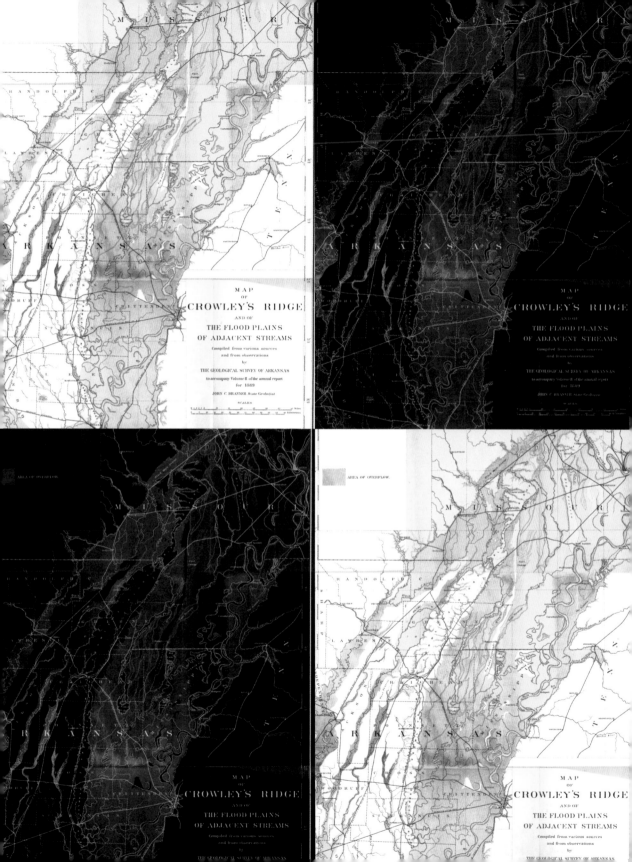

MAP
OF
CROWLEY'S RIDGE
AND OF
THE FLOOD PLAINS
OF ADJACENT STREAMS

Compiled from various sources
and from observations
by
THE GEOLOGICAL SURVEY OF ARKANSAS
to accompany Volume II of the annual report
for 1889

JOHN C. BRANNER, State Geologist

Beeches are quite singular in their winter appearance for two reasons. One is the distinctive bark—smooth, and silvery grey, with no wrinkles or furrows, no matter how old. (Beech crotches have always impressed me as the sexiest of any tree!) The other distinctive aspect is that in the winter, most younger, lower branches always hold on to a few of their dead leaves all winter. They have a distinctive parchment color, and when backlit transmit light. I love that about them. However, these leaves are dropped promptly as the spring buds expand.

The hanger-on-until-spring leaf is *marcescent.*

So noted by San Francisco–born Robert Frost:

We stood a moment so, in a strange world,
Myself as one his own pretense deceives;
And then I said the truth (and we moved on).
A young beech clinging to its last year's leaves.

This is why Milton is argued to have been mistaken when he wrote:

Thick as autumnal [beech] leaves that strow the brooks
In Vallombrosa, where th' Etrurian shades
High overarched embow'r; or scattered sedge
Afloat…

(It was a beech and fir forest surrounding the ancient Benedictine monastery at Vallombrosa, and if he visited at the reported time, the leaves should have still been clinging to their stems.)

George Herrick of Newport writes me that in *The Evolution of the Grand Tour*, Edward Chaney proposes that Milton could have borrowed his information from another source, probably Ariosto's *Orlando Furioso*.

All of Larry Lowman's information about beech aspect and behavior is borne out in the literature again and again, but there is nothing quite like a close encounter of the other kind, either at the elephant foot of one of the elder survivors of human disturbance and vengeful weather or from the mouth of a native plant master.

If you take root, the poet said to me, you'll go deep, C.D.
(Always the risk of becoming rootbound.)

A taproot is not the securing component of the beech, which instead spreads its elephantine feet out along the surface.

To be rooted is perhaps the most important and least recognized need of the human soul. Simone Weil, continuing: A human being has roots by virtue of his real, active and natural participation in the life of a community, which preserves in living shape certain particular treasures of the past and certain particular expectations for the future.

Minus the expectations, trees and humans do manifest a common gestalt.

Off Lick Branch trailhead on the Ozark Highlands Trail, the hollows are set by sandstone bluffs and tall beeches, understory of umbrella magnolias. The trail was handcrafted by volunteers, hikers to a person. While it was said to have been finished in 1984, ending at Norfork Lake, I have heard additional miles are being bushwhacked while I sink into the hollow of this canvas chair. I have not taken more than a mile or two of that hike, not having spent enough time in the hills since my parents died in 2009, but it makes the short list.

I propose the standing Wrights take an Ozark solidarity hike. Mother's friend Fern, a court reporter like herself, knows the hidden waterfalls of the hills, and while even Fern has gotten up there in dog years, it is hard to imagine her not being game. Fern grew up in a community ready-made for the construction of Norfork Dam. She was one of those dam kids.

Before the dam was built, Dad fished up a preposterously priapic rock in the riverbed, soon to be Norfork Lake. He stood the rock on the incinerator ledge with a fruit basket over it and treated it as an idol of baffling significance. I spent years trying to talk him out of the rock, but was only able to lay claim after he died.

(Your typical Wright is synchronously prudish and profane.)

~

After I reviewed Mr. Lowman's e-mail to my informant (excerpted above), I wrote back asking, *Who* is this guy.

Larry Lowman is an interesting guy. He used to be a naturalist for Village Creek State Park, and back in 1981 they instituted a dress code and told him he'd have to cut his long hair and ponytail. He refused, they fired him, and he filed suit against the state parks & tourism department and won in district court and again when the state appealed. Judge Henry Woods threw the case out and chewed out the state lawyers—"How dare you clog up my docket with such trivial stuff? Let this man get back to work."

Lowman ran a native plant nursery in Wynne for a long time and then got tired, as he put it, of having people ask him in the aisles of the grocery store about [his] being saved. Now he homesteads in Carroll County, off Hwy 21.

(He would have to drive from Berryville to Eureka Springs to dodge the same sectarian interrogation—and then, no guarantees—with the simple goal of stocking up on TP. He probably does.)

What I mean to say, trees and tree kin, each one a marvel unto themselves. No-nonsense judges have my respect as well. Henry Woods was that kind of lawman.

Prior to Mr. Lowman's guidance, I had been to Lost Valley twice. Once with my witty, no-nonsense father and a college friend from Brooklyn who went haywire when the first cloud of gnats showed up—it was worthy of Woody Allen, whose crew reportedly had to douse him with Evian water when the scene called for Woody appearing to be emerging from a pond.

The next trip was with my husband (Forrest) and son (Brecht) whom I was seasonally trying to woo to hill-country splendor (I knew it was not going to be the lure of local grammar, dental work, or cookery). I was not beech-conscious at the time. Before we reached the turn-off, we passed a motorcycle tree. Shoe trees and blue-bottle trees are not uncommon on country roads, but it is exceptional to find a tree hung with someone's broken-down choppers. Burdensome for the stoic oak. A dude ranch had been built in the heart of Lost Valley, and polychromatic-puffy-jacketed rock climbers dotted the calico face of the bluffs. The valley still offers up its unwelcome nets of gnats.

~

This amble began with a low-on-the-Janka-scale nightmare: I am learning to play the piccolo. I am officially enrolled in a piccolo class, but I am not keeping up with the assignments, my embouchure is lousy, and I am panting around town frantically hitting up the three people I know from class to try to snag the last assignment. The approach of a final recital turns my hair cotton-white. My fellow players are supposed to be friends, but they have had it with my lame level of responsibility. Now I am scrambling all over campus trying to see whether I can drop the class so I don't get a big fat hairy *F.* The registrar has already closed shop. My last hope is the *maestra,* but I cannot, I cannot face her now. This is not that interesting, just enervating, and I am sure it is tangential to signing on to write about beeches.

As a by-product of the Ozark Mountains, I have long been at least semi-aware of my standing brothers and sisters, the hardwoods. Rocks, rivers, and trees we had in surplus. In our yard were four species of oak—white, post, blackjack, and Arkansas oak (there are 29 species in the state); 7 or 9 pink and white dogwoods, a handsome blue spruce, an A1 southern magnolia, and two cedar sentinels beside the front steps. The red maple we lost early on.

The oak (*Quercus*) is of the same family as the beech (Fagaceae), as is the chestnut (*Castanea*). And the chinkapin (*Castanopsis*) that gets it on with both oak and chestnut. The chinkapin's only native hails from Oregon, or so they say; however, there is an Ozark Chinquapin (*Castanea ozarkensis*) related to the chestnut and fallen to the same blight as the American chestnut (*Castanea dentata*)—reduced in most parts of the land to root suckers producing few seeds.

An initiative to save the chinkapin has begun to establish three orchards in southwest Missouri. The poet Deborah Digges (née Sugarbaker), one of ten siblings, daughter of an oncologist and prison minister (also orchardists), grew up in that corner of Missouri. We grew up within three hours and two years of each other. I never met her, but when she jumped from a stadium in Amherst I felt that I had been her familiar. I cannot say I felt her fall. I felt her struggle against that terminus. A tree is a resilient fighter. Likewise poets, single mothers, and teachers. Not every struggle can be overcome. The effort is usually drawn-out and gutsy. I think of singer/songwriter Vic Chesnutt often. His friends conspired to spare him. The world did not. Once off the respirator there wasn't time for a single sip of air.

(East of the Mississippi, forget about the American chestnut.)

Horse chestnuts aplenty; contrary to an old potion, not in the least beneficial to the horse's chest. Native to the Mediterranean. Not even an actual chestnut, more like a cousin 4th removed. Japanese and Chinese chestnuts are common and resistant to the blight the Japanese stock introduced. So it goes. The California chestnut is in fact the bisexual buckeye (native to Northern California and southwest Oregon).

The chinkapin succumbed. I remember eating them on a 9-hole golf course when my father espied one in the rough where our balls forlornly lay. Couple of born duffers. I curse-swished Spaldings at age 10, but I was excited by the sweet mini nut in the spiny shell.

Or was it a pawpaw tree. One thing I can certify, it was in southwest Missouri and there were pocket gophers; we stopped under a tree Dad recognized and we ate of its nut or fruit.

I know I ate of the pawpaw one time only. I remember a cross-between-an-apple-and-banana flavor with the more-banana-than-apple texture. I know I was with Dad or it would have never occurred to me to put such an ugly object in my mouth. Now some scientist has made it attractive, but it has not fallen under Monsanto's gluttonous reach to date.

~

My folks were not yard people and by the time we moved again the spruce had lost its pointed head, then its tented body; the cedars were sagging with bagworms and the dogwoods looking pretty doggy; and at least 5 of the oaks had been felled. No climbing trees since Mother was vigilant of anyone getting up in the magnolia, and the oaks had no lower limbs. I did have a long-chained tree swing on one of the big oaks, and I made up many a wandering off-key song as the monarchs flitted around me and I pumped my bony legs to go higher. When one of the chains broke, a tire swing had to serve as no one was going up the big tree to hang another chain. Dank water often sloshed in the bottom of the tire up against my shorts. The dogwoods were squat, flouncy things, and I thought

of them on my level as if they were other children. The spirea, forsythia, and japonica disappeared along with the climbing roses, the tulips, and spreading beds of thrift. We should have left in shame, but the parents relocated and destroyed other less notable lots around their successive houses.

For Christmas we were committed to the red cedar. Dad would drive down a random dirt road or two-lane highway until he spied a loner outside a fence line. Or just inside (easy to jump the fence if a bull came charging). He thought it was stupid to buy a tree, and viewed them as common property. One year I nagged him into flocking the tree, and I readily call up the slapstick sight of him pinning the top of the tree to the clothesline and spraying phony snow from an aerosol canister in a big wind, cussing like the country soul he was, while he flocked himself and the hapless cedar for the first and last time. Then the poor freakish-looking thing was mounted at a tilt in a minnow bucket full of rocks with Mother's unfinished felt tree skirt bunched up around it. Once both my brother and I had left home, the parents settled on an aluminum tree Mother left up year-round adorned with uniform ice-blue balls.

Another minor tree-related matter was that I was very nearsighted. So much so that the tall trees were impressionistic creations to my eyes. Their leaves individuated upon whirling to the ground or upon my climbing to their level.

(The buds of tree consciousness.)

One of my early tree infatuations was associated with a sternly aristocratic, white stucco house on Hwy 7 en route to the Buffalo River for a swim. A house named Twelve Oaks. The drive lined with a dozen imposing oaks. A tornado took each one of them out like soda straws. Without them the house looked like an asylum. Exactly like an asylum.

~

The famous upside-down tree (*Fagus sylvatica* 'Pendula') in London's Hyde Park is not nearly so wowing as the one at Colt State Park in Bristol, RI (same town where Blithewold Arboretum is situated), from which I flushed an entire human family when I slipped under its alluring limbs and into their obscure encampment. The Rhode Island park was a former farm bought by the state from "Pom" Colt, brother of the gun maker, himself an advocate for child labor laws and women's property rights, and a moneymaking man, founder of a trust company that in its latest incarnation merged with Bank of America; also president of a rubber company that in its latest incarnation became Uniroyal.

Under the *Fagus sylvatica* 'Pendula' at Arnold Arboretum, I found the leftover tins and odd articles of clothing of the tree's former denizens, before winter exposed their hideaway.

After a reading with poets Forrest Gander and Víctor Rodríguez Núñez at London Review Bookshop, a small band of us went to dinner. I sat next to a shy, courteous man named William. When I learned he lived near the Chiltern Woodlands I asked him about the beech trees, and he asked whether I knew, regarding the American West, about the glory hole under beeches. Because the trees fall over, he said, there was rumored to be the phenomenon of finding gold nuggets in the cavities exposed by their toppling. Eureka! (Which Archimedes is attributed to have been the first to exclaim, running naked with excitement through the streets of Syracuse, having lit upon the principle of hydrostatics.)

I admitted to my dinner partner I knew nothing about gold being discovered under blowdown beeches, but alerted him that glory hole had an entirely different connotation in the US, and he wouldn't want to bring up the subject with just anybody. (I later learned the term *can* refer to alluvial gold mining pockets in old riverbeds or at the foot of waterfalls.)

Later yet, I stumbled upon a tale about an Arkansas farmer in Pope Co. gone to check on his corn in the bottomland off of Big Piney Creek (not far from Okay, AR) coming across a couple of murky characters who approached him to ask whether he knew of any rocks around there with turtles etched on them. The next day he saw the same pair of strangers in a wagon of tools pulled by a gaunt horse, shotguns across their laps, looking less neighborly than on first encounter. After they had departed he and his boy found their campsite close to a beech tree with a carving of a snake, head pointed downward, on its trunk and a hole dug out around the tree. Not far from that they found a rock with a turtle carved on it. The tale had passed down that the Spaniards used emblems of serpents and turtles to mark buried treasure. (I always had the impression the 16th-century conquistadores would sooner leave behind their firstborn than their gold. A diamond mine in the state has yielded a handful of get-rich-quickers, but gold prospecting has never been regarded a productive Arkansas operation.)

~

It was not until I began living in cities that I became hypercognizant of the landscape I had left. Come spring I experienced a visceral absence: where were the oaks and hickories; the walnuts from which it looked as if pterodactyls might swoop down and haul off a squealing child; the uncommon pawpaws; red maples and cottonwoods, serviceberry, dogwoods, and redbuds, red cedars, and pines (in which I was least interested); the lawns of magnolias, and crab apples that could pollinate a Black apple, the Arkansas Black Winesap being the best apple on this whole green globe (but not to be planted near a walnut). And where were all those showy flowering bushes like japonica and forsythia and spirea and lilacs, lace-cap hydrangea and shrub roses.

Speaking of lilacs:
Mother buried the poodle under the lilac in her Santa Claus suit of which she thought the dog was fond (the suit not the bush). She further convinced herself that the dog took her own life when she overheard Mother saying if her allergies worsened she might have to give the dog away, prompting Puddles to run out the front door instead of the back, her usual exit. Mother was not in the least crazy, but she had a naive streak she maintained through the best and worst of times.

When I found a sick squirrel in the backyard, I dressed it in doll clothes and tucked it under a blankie in my doll buggy parked next to my bed overnight, only to waken to a stiffened corpse with bared teeth and seized-up claws. When I returned from school, looking forward to adding it to my pet cemetery, Dad told me he had respectfully cremated it, meaning he burned it in the brick grill where we barbecued our wieners.

~

In Memphis there are estate-sized magnolias. In New York City, the squirrels and the trees both look pretty beat, though Central Park in the rain can still feel restorative. In San Francisco, there are the towering eucalyptuses and profuse rhododendrons in Golden Gate Park, palms on Dolores and at the Artaud theater, New Zealand bottlebrushes, and streetside strawberry trees. In Dolores Hidalgo, state of Guanajuato, the flamboyanes and jacarandas and mesquites and my first pomegranate in the courtyard of the Museo Casa de Hidalgo. (While Miguel Hidalgo's bell-tolling alarm and great grita de Dolores are credited with inaugurating their revolution, he was in much deeper than that. The good padre was a full-fledged motivator of the revolt, for which his head was displayed on a spike in Guanajuato.)

It is also written of Dolores Hidalgo that a tree grown from sapling from the Árbol de la Noche Triste, a Montezuma cypress (*Ahuehuete*), stands in the main plaza. It celebrates Cortés's defeat in the Aztec revolt in 1520. However, Montezuma died in the fight, and Cortés escaped by the hair of his chinny chin chin. When living in Dolores Hidalgo, I enjoyed the company of an outstanding tree in the plaza and the ruction of oversized birds that weighted down its limbs in the evening while my beloved and I chomped on charcoaled corn rubbed with red pepper and lime juice.

Then there is the Montezuma cypress, El Árbol del Tule, in Santa María del Tule, Oaxaca. Words don't come close. Never have. Never will.

Were I a diviner of children's books, I would compose a multigenerational Gongorismo chronicle from the point of view of the creatures who have burrowed, nested, and sported in the shelter of that spectacular tree, somewhere between 1,400 and 3,000 years old (opinions differ). I would have to consume many a magic mushroom to touch the wonder.

Second Monday of October el Árbol is given a party.

El Árbol del Tule enjoys the title of the world's fattest.

In the USA, we the people enjoy the title of the world's fattest.

Water
      is an issue
Pollution
      is an issue
The table
      is dropping
The cars
      they are
breeding

Sometimes nothing to do but gawk. Openmouthed. Bug-eyed. Gobsmacked.

ART IS SEEING WHAT YOU HAVEN'T FELT BEFORE

DENNY MOERS

When C.D. called to ask me about photographing beech trees for a book she was working on, I did not confess to her that I didn't know the difference between a beech and a birch. This was confirmed when she dispatched me up to Mt. Auburn Cemetery to photograph the beech tree beside Robert Creeley's gravesite. I had a bit of a row with the admin office as I insisted that they had birch trees there and they insisted they did not. But after that day, I fell deeply for our glorious beech trees and forever am I grateful to C.D. for tapping me awake to see what she was seeing.

Beech trees are a magnificent brood. Their massive grey trunks conjure up elephant skin, and their size and unique attributes add feelings that one is among a herd of majestic creatures. When one experiences a complete grove of European beeches, it is like a life force revealed.

During a snowstorm or on a hot summer day, C.D. would ring up and we'd strike out to see a select lot of these creatures that she knew or wanted to know. Sometimes we went just to see their roots. Once we set out with my daughter to see a magnificent tree C.D. had written about, but it was no longer there. It had been taken down to earth level. It was a shattering loss, as though a dear friend had just been listed among the disappeared.

My photographic process is rooted in the black-and-white darkroom and the notion that each individual sheet of photographic paper is sensitized to light and chemicals and can contain a multitude of emotions and concepts. This notion of working stems from Charles Olson and his "composition by field" notes. With light, developer, fixer, and gold and selenium toners, I work directly on each sheet of paper (thus the concept of monoprints). I often apply chemistry with powder and spray all selectively applied. I seek to transform from the literal to the imagined with accident and design vying for my attention.

One night C.D. came over in a bit of a panic. She needed to know whether I was going to "do my mojo thing" on the pictures I was taking, that I wasn't planning to present her with just black-and-white prints. I reassured her that she would get her mojo as desired. Later on, after the prints started appearing from my darkroom, I felt that perhaps they were coming out too dark and I might be missing another side to things. She answered that she always liked things dark and dirty and not to worry about it. Solid advice.

Since *Tremble*, C.D. has used several of my monoprints for her book covers. I realize now that the cover photo we chose for *Tremble* was as singular a tree as any of the beech trees I photographed for her years later. Her eye was unerring and utterly perceptive. As I lived but a few blocks away, I would often drop by quite unannounced. In my life, there was nothing so exciting as beginning a conversation with C.D. It was like a fix, a jolt, an unerring revealing of the truth no matter what. The last time I saw her before her trip to South America, she said, "When I get back I want to go see some roots that I heard about, okay?" Yes, okay.

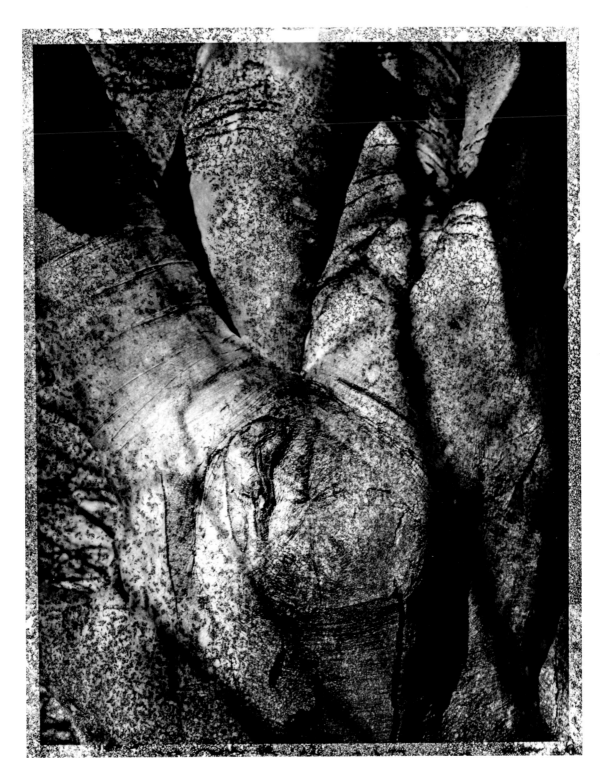

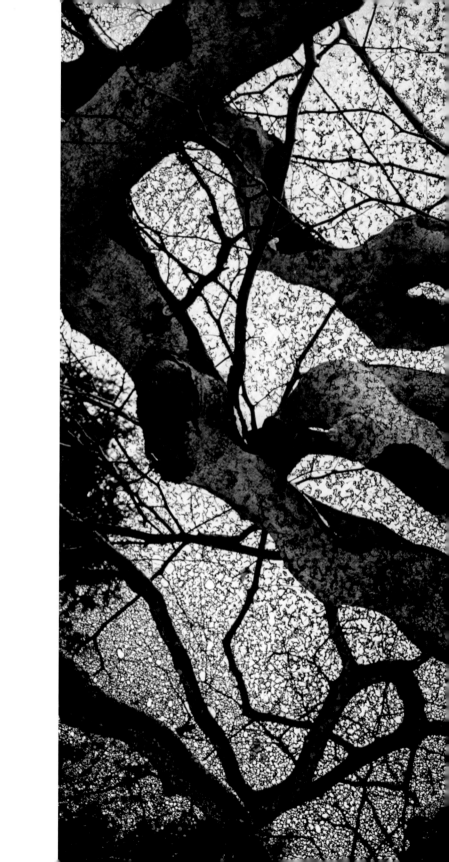

~

When we moved to Rhode Island, I wondered where all the trees had gone. Houses tended to consume their entire lots in Providence, and bushes grew flush against brick or clapboard, often shorn to look as if they had been reared up in molds.

When we moved from a loft downtown (where, gradually we caught on, few others chose to live), we bought a solid forties house across from Roger Williams Park. Immediately opposite us, on the wide median of a park road, stood a neofascistic-looking statue of an eagle made by a well-intentioned young artist. Its setting has since been replaced by a slender, muscular bronze falconer hauled out of storage. The park was on the shaggy side but had a great variety of trees, including a magnificent London plane the maintenance crew had the foresight to cable. After the baby was born, I became abruptly and keenly cognizant of the drug dealers on the next block.

Next door to us lived an elderly Republican lady, distant, friendly, and offensive, by turn.

Her side yard was overshadowed by a copper beech. It rose above her three-story brick fortress. She said her father had planted it when she was a small girl, when it stood daffodil-tall.

When she told us she suspected the darkies of having stolen her copper drain pipes, my eyes snapped, in the way of my father's before me. *Someone* stole her drain pipes. *Darkies* I had not heard outside of Uncle Remus tales and *Gone with the Wind*. I often stared at the tree when strolling the baby whom the neighbor dubbed a fresh-air baby; passing the beech with a mix of sympathy and antipathy I had transferred from her to the innocent tree. To me, it was a new tree, weighed down with a misdirected superiority.

~

Average height: about 120 feet
Canopy: 70 feet
On the Janka scale of hardness: 1,300.

Measuring softness or hardness, it's high. Ultra hard is 4,000. Brazilian walnut and ebony are up there.

1,300, meaning the wood is fit for flooring. Being acquainted with a number of these individuals now, I don't like the thought of walking on them in my dirt-caked Dingoes.

Not an easy wood to stain. Says one.

Easy to stain, says another.

Don't use on the bathroom floor. Can handle total submersion but not the wet/dry, wet/dry treatment. A summer flooding could kill it outright, a winter, not so likely.

Though it does not weather well as timber, it survives being submerged in water—why it was used for waterwheels and keels of wooden ships.

Fagus sylvatica, the European beech, has many cultivars, depending upon your source. Scores of variants on those.

The European beeches like it here, but the American beeches don't like it there.

Fagus grandifolia, the American beech, has no cultivars, no variety.

He/she is on his/her own.

He/she is not an ornamental.

Alone, has been referred to as a pasture tree.

An American's heartwood is dark.

~

Fagus has long been thought to derive from Greek, *phaegein:* to eat. The disagreement is that *bhago* is of Indo-European origin for both "beech" and "trees."

First page
        of literature
in Sanskrit
        on beech
the runic tablets
        on beech
First books
        were beech
in Sanskrit
        the Vedas
who knows
        who wrote
Old English
        on bound
beech
        bark

Beech is Anglo-Saxon *bóc:* book, document, or charter; and *beche* in Middle English, *bech, beetch, beeche* from Old English; *bēce* of Germanic origin, *buoh* in Old High German, *boke* in Middle Low German, *baike* in Modern Low German, in modern German *Buche,* Old Norse *bok,* and Dutch *boek* and Danish *bøg* and Swedish *bok,* all meaning both book and beech; Latin *fagus,* Greek *phēgos:* esculent oak. Also *bog, buk,* and *buke.* Indo-European is *bhes gos.*

I have always wanted to call up my own first shimmer of printed-word recognition, of actually making out a simple sentence. I remember learning to tie my shoe on the bottom stair step of the house on South Cherry Street, the old farmhouse, by then in the middle of town, clad in pink asbestos shingles. Rushing up the stairs to wake the parents with the breaking news, with which they were less than ecstatic given the hour of the occasion, but by then I was already a reader. Already printing, leaving notes on the tree stump for the next-door neighbor. Our common paper was 8½" × 11" glossy fan photos of baseball players blank on the back side. My neighbor's father had a clankety Multilith press in his basement. I liked to imagine he forged the autographs on the pictures and sold them, and that he got stinking rich doing so. I sincerely aspired to be living next door to a celebrity forger.

I liked roller skates and walking dolls and crayons and long-haired cats and books. I sometimes had ringworms from adopted strays. I loved opening the book wide and close to my nearsighted face. I took pride in maxing out my library card and checking out titles deemed beyond my understanding. I was loath to close the book. I would color in Olan Mills's studio photographs of my parents, but never colored in books. Aside from abusing my single pop-up book, I never vandalized a book.

Mother Goose was the first book. A pop-up from Mamo and Bapo. I pulled out most of the pop-ups except for the four-and-twenty blackbirds from the King's pie. I learned the rhymes by heart, but did I read them? The closest I come to recollecting that transformative moment is an eventual drift of attention away from the overly familiar images to the brazen, cryptic black letters.

One Gordon Saltar at Winterthur and the Royal Forestry Commission in England identified the presence of tandem rays and crystals in the American variety which aren't found in European beeches. I don't know when, though he is referred to as a pioneer; Winterthur is in Delaware. Unshockingly, the estate of one Henry Algernon du Pont. Henry started out making watches in Paris, re-started making gunpowder in America. Ensued a string of intermarrying cousins; thus, a Delaware chemical fiefdom of dubious distinction.

~

Fagus Deus, god of the beech tree, Gallo-Roman. Inscribed in the Pyrenees by the Aquitaines. The Celts adopted him, but mistletoe and non-beech trees were by far preferred.

In Rome, Jupiter was worshipped in a beech sanctuary on one of the seven hills, the Esquiline, under the name of Jupiter Fagutalis, also Phegone, meaning, inhabitant of a beech tree. The beech at Dodona was regarded as an oracle, whence Jupiter got his mail. Another at Tusculum was dedicated to Diana.

Celts had cults of trees, oak esp but also beech and yew trees, worshipped in conjunction with wells and springs. That vile green man oracle, a beech, derives from some of this occultism. In illustrations, he is always erupting vegetation from one or usually more than one orifice. The Christians adapted him to their own cravings and carvings.

The sulfur-reeking green man enters the 19th-century Swiss story by Rev. Jeremias Gotthelf of a cruel knight who cannot take enough out on his servants. Having built him a castle, and still being forced to harvest on time and pay taxes in full, the servants are now charged to bring a hundred Münneberg beech trees, a woods three days off, and plant them in a row beside his castle. Only a deal with the devil would make this possible, and only one bold woman in the village thinks she can outwit the Evil One. In exchange for the beech trees' being delivered (by flaming squirrels) to the castle, an unbaptized child must be turned over to the green man. Small price for a fine avenue of beeches. For now the story's progress continues without us.

It is said that Crispus (who married the empress euphoniously named Agrippina) poured wine on the roots of a beech and often wrapped himself around its bole.

It is said that Apollo and Athena, having been turned into repulsive vultures, sat in a beech and watched the Greeks and Trojans battle.

~

Quia olim homines fructibus arboreis victitabant: Because once upon a time men fed on mast.

Where I have found mast, squirrels *et al.* have raided the cupules, beat me to the nut.

The nuts are a touch toxic, yet edible, and were food for us alongside filling the bellies of hogs and squirrels, white-footed mice, pheasants, grouse, deer, black bears, and the doomed carrier pigeon. More down the line on that violently disappeared beauty.

Heat kills the toxin. Or a good soaking leaches the tannins.

The first bread from beech flour.

~

I have never heard it defamed as a hanging tree.

~

Outside my Rhode Island study stands a red cedar (*Juniperus virginiana*), an asymmetrical, multiple amputee, once rightfully named the pencil tree, displaced by the columnar incense cedar (*Calocedrus*) out West when the supply of red thinned out back East. I have heard tell of the cedar being planted to guard a grave.

In the burial ground bordering our Rhode Island yard, gum trees keep watch over the headstones. One of the older pair of stones has lichened up, fallen over, and broken into several chunks belonging to a Lucy J. / Wife of Edwin L. Martin / Died Dec 25, 1875 / Aged 26 years & 6 months. Edith F. / Their Daughter / Died Dec 26, 1875 / Aged 5 months; Edwin L. Martin / Died June 12, 1884 / Aged 35 years / 9 months & 1 day. (One lonesome, achy-hearted Christmas spent by Edwin L. who lived a funeral nine years more.)

~

Texans, it is written by a Texan, regard a tree as a fence post in the rough. Who needs a shade tree when you've got a big hat? The best way to survive as a tree in Texas is to arrange to have some historic event occur under your branches. Beeches don't grow in west Texas and are declining in east Texas as it gets hotter and hotter.

~

Preglacially, they flourished all over North America. N/S, E/W.

They love humus. Hillsides. Slopes. Edges.

They like to be within earshot of water.   Louis the Plant Geek

Also observes the golden-leaved weeper is reserved in its weeping ways.

In the West they like the alkali from clam shells.

Even when old, look young. Good-looking throughout their passage.

Whereas your oaks tend to look older than their age. (Ditto the Wrights.)

~

A carving tree:

        Or shall I rather the sad verse repeat
Which on the beech's bark I lately writ?   Virgil

(Some say it had to be the chestnut of which he spoke. Same outsize family.)

~

The beech bears the scars of love: Erica loves Ricky, Julia loves Jesus. "Better to propose marriage at Yankee Stadium by dirigible than to carve initials into a beech," suggests one would-be protector.

Mitch Epstein's photographs of New York's landmark trees include a beech tattooed from toe to crown. One of those deeds that cannot be undone.

For its carving: autograph tree, initial tree, scarring tree, tattoo tree, valentine tree:

> O Rosalind, these trees shall be my books,
> And in their barks my thoughts I'll character,
> That every eye which in this forest looks
> Shall see thy virtue witness'd every where.
> Run, run, Orlando, carve on every tree
> The fair, the chaste, and unexpressive she.

Who [shall] grave on the rind of my smooth beeches some belovèd name? William Cullen Bryant. Dad was appreciative of Bryant. I could not comprehend this. He chose a selection from Bryant for "The Lost Roads Project," reading a passage on immortality, from his courtroom bench in his frayed robes, filmed by my husband, Forrest. My father's voice by then fragile as a moth wing. My husband wore Dad's robes at commencements at Brown until they fell apart.

Among the most famous of the signed specimens (from the literary angle) stands at Coole Park, Lady Gregory's estate, signed by Yeats of course, Shaw, O'Casey, Synge, and all the other Irish hotshot writers of the day.

Maud Gonne never loved poor William Butler Yeats, though I can't believe she ever fell for the creepy major she married, whom quickly in fact she loved not. Poor WB proposed to Maud's daughter Iseult, conceived in her dead brother's mausoleum from MG's liaison with a married Frenchman. Since Yeats couldn't have Maud... I think he should have lost his virginity at a far earlier age. But then we would have been deprived of the frustration his ear alone sustained with grace.

Coole House no longer stands, but the copper beech near Gort which Lady Gregory encouraged her guests to autograph lives on.

And it was "a beechen green" wherein Keats's "light-winged Dryad," the nightingale, sang "in full-throated ease."

I happened on a mention that Europeans once regarded a copper in the wild as a mark of nature's censure for some unnatural offense; therefore, suggested planting in moderation.

For a carving, the Bible Tree, near Brookville, PA, scripture inscribed by a hermit as instructed in a vision.

For healing, esp asthma in a child: core out a hole in trunk, put lock of asthmatic's hair in hole. Plug hole. When child has reached height of hole, asthma will be all gone.

My brother had warts on his hands he was told were transmitted by frog urine (perhaps a rural Protestant ersatz penance for masturbation). Grandma Wright rubbed the warts with bean leaves. Instructed Warren to bury the leaves and never look back. When this did not prove effective, he had the warts burned off at the doc's office. Grandma Wright said he looked back. He insisted he had not. Then you didn't believe. She snapped her eyes.

On the weeping beech Epstein photographed in Brooklyn's Botanic Garden, *Heaven* is knifed into its uppermost reaches.

Indian Tree, because it does not take to "civilized" conditions.

For its carving, a witness tree: I think of a witness tree as one that stood its ground, when something happened, possibly something no human was meant to see. I think of the Pacific yew in Warren, RI, brought over on one of Commodore Perry's black ships by the botanists Rev. Samuel Williams and Dr. James Morrow. In 1978 a murder took place in the severe old house on Miller Street with its side-yard yew. Midday, the victim, owner of the emporium, House of a Million Items, was in the shower. Ten shots to the abdomen and the temple. That's hatred. Cold and bloody.

(The bark of the Pacific yew [*Taxus brevifolia*] was discovered to be the natural source of paclitaxel [Taxol], but the cancer-fighting compound required 2 tons of bark to yield 10 pure grams. Eventually a "blockbuster" synthetic was developed in lieu of yew bark.)

A probable, never-charged patricide. A botched investigation, contaminated evidence, a cover-up, and so forth. When I pass the house, I see the yew long risen past the window on the second floor I picture being the site of the attack on a naked, nearsighted man.

Witness tree, graffiti tree, tattoo tree, autograph tree, trysting tree, avenue tree, arborglyph, CMT (culturally modified tree), Presidents' Tree (for the one in Takoma Park carved with presidents from Washington to Lincoln in 1865; blown down in 1997). They say it really doesn't hurt the tree, all that carving. But harm and hurt are different. Beech bark is a tender thing.

In Bankhead National Forest, AL, there are many message trees, including one of the horned serpent Uktena.

So Tennyson sat on a "serpent-rooted beech."

X meant HONEY HERE. It still means honey here.

Honey, *if* the bees be with us.

(If we go, *says the cartoon bee's speech bubble,* we're taking you with us.)

As one scientist put it, *We* are the asteroid.

Knowing the general outline of argument of the Holocene extinction put forth by Elizabeth Kolbert in *The Sixth Extinction: An Unnatural History,* I have not yet brought myself to the pain of cracking its spine, to be taken to the brink. I sit here eating "carefully watched over" cashews grown in India, from one of the 102 billion plastic bags used annually in the US, wearing a linen shirt (albeit secondhand) made in China, jeans fabriqué en Haïti, Delta Blues Museum T-shirt made in Honduras… a walking, talking profligate. I once crouched in the Cortona cell where the mendicant Saint Francis spent his last deathward winter, and his no-thermostat-coarse-wool-tunic demise is not an alternative I would choose, but the pressing necessity of conserving resources, curbing consumption, functioning in an economy shifted closer to the source gathers force with each extinguished specimen.

Never fear, RoboBees are coming to your clover and climbing roses soon, courtesy of Micro Air Vehicles Project at Harvard. Never fear, W.S. Merwin assured, there is a hair hanging by everything / it is the edges of things.

In the meantime, hand-pollinating with tiny brushes or cotton swabs is on the rise.

~

Regarding the witness tree:
Beech is preferred for carving in the East, aspen in the West.

Sequoyah Cemetery in the Smokies contains one fieldstone inscribed in the syllabary, but I have not turned up a nondisputed example of an extant beech tree using the Cherokee's system.

Sequoyah, meaning "pig's foot," reputedly nicknamed by his father for an injury that left him lame. Within a year of finishing his 86-symbol syllabary in 1821, Sequoyah's legacy was secure: a whopping 90 percent of the Cherokee Nation was reputed to be literate by the time the *Cherokee Phoenix* was in the middle of its 6-year print run.

According to a 2013 study by the US Dept of Education and the National Institute of Literacy, 14 percent of our population cannot read, 21 percent of adults read below a 5th-grade level, and 19 percent of high school graduates cannot read.

The *Cherokee Phoenix* was first published in New Echota (near Calhoun, GA) in 1828. Signage on the trees was common. Some of these arborglyphs still endure, so I am told. Should there be any from that time, their lettering would obviously be far from the ground and much blurred from expanding with the tree's growth.

Sequoyah is alleged to have kept notebooks on his last journey, into northeastern Mexico, a quest undertaken to account for each living Cherokee soul. The cave in which he was stove-up, too weak to travel farther, flooded before his son and other followers returned to find his body; his saddlebags washed away, including his priceless notebooks.

Sequoyah's notebooks: this document would come closer to a sacred text for me than the Constitution (however subverted by the current Court-of-last-resort's majority). Other accounts have the Cherokee Cadmus breathing his last in San Fernando, Mexico, saddlebags and papers having been retrieved downstream from the cave. No one has yet to come forward with a scrap.

Beech trees on the Trail of Tears are marked by Cherokee in presyllabaric code (Sequoyah stopped in Arkansas at a spot near Greers Ferry, now underwater, where he finished his single-minded opus).

The color for the Long Hair Clan of Cherokee (also known as Twister, Wind, or Hanging Down Clan) is yellow. Their tree is beech.

~

The beeches of Oradell, NJ, are said to have witnessed certain episodes of the American Revolutionary War. Many trees went down, but the beeches survived the nor'easter of 2010, Hurricane Irene, and Superstorm Sandy.

~

Haverford College campus in Philadelphia's Main Line is an arboretum, 200 acres. The grounds were designed in the Reptonian manner after the 18th-century English landscaper Humphry Repton by the English gardener William Carvell (who also introduced cricket to the US). Most of the trees on campus are marked. It hosts 13 state-champion trees. They have 5 varieties of beech; I took the tree walk provided by a map, in the wrong shoes as usual, snowmelt packing my socks. The campus has 5 species of beech, and though one of them gives the arboretum director fits, messing with the symmetry and the sightlines, it is young and will have a chance to haul up its canopy.

A pair of fine American beeches I had not previously encountered as landscape trees creates an entrance to Stokes Hall; the rest of their beeches are European. Given the grounds themselves constitute an arboretum, variety is part and parcel of the mandate.

Still speaking of witness trees: Haverford has an elm (*Ulmus americana*) of which they are particularly proud, the Penn Treaty Elm, a scion of the elm from the banks of the Delaware where William Penn signed a friendship treaty with Lenape (Delaware) Chief Tamanend. Now the original witness tree on the Delaware has been replaced with a scion from Haverford. I can't help but feel goodwill toward the treating of trees and their descendants as honorable "participants" of historical dramas. Voltaire said it was the only treaty, the only one never signed and never broken. (Since Penn was a Quaker he was forbidden to sign oaths, but apparently bound to abide by them. It seems pretty whitewashed, but one badly wants to believe some weighty promise has held.)

~

Now that I am in California for a few months, my attention is easily diverted by the live oaks, redwoods, sycamores, junipers, cypresses, pines, yews, firs, buckeyes. At the ranch of a friend I said a bit about the beech and she asked whether any grew around here. She knows her trees. I said they didn't like the salt in the air or the soil, and I said I didn't expect to see a beech in California. Her carpenter said, "Everything grows in California." Almost: there is that wild-looking bunya-bunya (false monkey puzzle tree) in front of the historical museum. I don't know what it thinks it's doing here. The cones weigh 10 pounds (the size of bocce balls); so if you are walking under the drop zone at the wrong moment, you will be taking the long-term dirt nap.

I don't know the difference between the false and true monkey puzzle, except the true is from Chile and the false from Australia, and the former is endangered. They have been around since the late Permian, 250 million years.

Thinking of exotics: I was driving a big-finned DeSoto back from the Arkansas Delta. It broke down in Salem, AR. A bona fide shade tree mechanic towed that cruise ship of an automobile to his airplane hangar after he got home from the stock car races. Once it became obvious I was not going anywhere anytime fast, a policeman drove me to the station, and then to a motel run by a nice widow lady. It was a timing-chain job. I remember a cork tree in front of the library. Could have been the only one in the state. The only cork tree I ever clapped eyes on. Not so impressive but different enough to my way of seeing I had to inquire at the checkout desk, What is that freaky-looking tree out front.

~

I texted a poet in New York who grew up in California. Her late mother's Berkeley house had a beech tree in the front. She sent the address on Tanglewood Rd; I Google-Earthed and zoomed in. There she/he was. Privacy is an easily perverted issue. You can create a record you do not want, no matter how good you are going forward. You can pay to eradicate a record you did not want, no matter how ruthless you have been and will be going forward. You can invent a convincing case history. For the moment, I can locate you, whosoever you are, or re-imagine you in a keystroke. I can see the tree that cast your lawn in deep shade when you were wearing a linen dress, a string of seed pearls, and no underpants.

There are some coppers living in Berkeley, sometimes as a street tree, which is a wicked thing to do to a *Fagus sylvatica* 'Cuprea'.

Still, California beech trees in my North Bay environment were looking unlikely. I took off on a slo-mo neighborhood run the morning the track and bleachers were streaming and screaming through their high school graduation ceremony. When I plugged a ways down I Street, I spotted one. Not just one of the few cultivars I have seen so many of, but a tricolor ('Roseomarginata'). Lacking the full supplement of chlorophyll, a delicate pink trimming the leaf. I come back later on my scooter and talk briefly to the owner. She tells me they have lived there for 30 years. They came from the Midwest. The tricolor was about as big around as an ankle bracelet when they moved in. Now it is 3-footish in circumference. It would be bigger if not hemmed in by the neighbor's driveway and three big buckeyes. The owner keeps it pruned and inoculated against beech blight aphids (*Grylloprociphilus imbricator*) that also encourage a fungus, a sooty mold (*Scorias spongiosa*). For good measure the aphids poop honeydew, bringing on the ants.

(Yet another encounter yesterday, on a hike up to the trails behind us, a large stucco house embalmed on the hillside with a small fortune in plantings, including a purple fountain and a purple beech arch. They are young. A little time will tell whether they can manage the environment.)

(And another at the Luther Burbank home and garden in Santa Rosa. He developed hundreds of plants, including a spineless cactus to feed cattle. The one in his garden is as big as a shed. Many yummy fruits, russet potatoes, hearty grasses, and the Shasta daisy, a quadruple hybrid, were of his making. He was absorbed, sweet as a plumcot [also his creation], easy on the eyes, and a copper beech continues to extend its lovely limbs across his front yard. Everything grows in California.)

The owner of the tricolor on I Street said people used to stop on occasion and request a small branch for some sort of celebration. No, they were told, you cannot go breaking branches off that tree and don't come back at night because I know your face. What kind of pagan business would entail removing limbs from the only tree of its kind around.

A minimal search turns up: Use a beech branch as a wand to open channels for communication with spirits and gods/goddesses. It will enable you to quickly draw down divine energy into your circle. Californians are given to making wands of branches. The woman who cuts my hair said a friend of hers was earning big enough money with her smudging feathers to quit her regular job. This would be ill-advised back East.

∼

Toronto, June 3, 2014:

(I must first acknowledge the 36th anniversary of the death of poet Frank Stanford. As a land surveyor he took a chainsaw to many a tree in the dense woods of the Ozarks. His friend Willett would often be furious with him if he didn't know what he was taking down before revving up.) But jogging in the park, at my sluggish tempo, near the hotel, I slammed smack-dab into a pretty copper. I wanted to pluck just one leaf (I am an addicted plucker, self-limiting to one leaf). The one I happened to flip over was wall-to-wall with the beech blight aphid (*G. imbricator*). Their sole self-defense is to raise their hind ends and sway in unison. *Little fuckers.**

---

* "Little Fucker[s]" is also the title of a song by Vic Chesnutt and Elf Power. Also known as "LFs."

In Toronto, I met a physically vulnerable, emotionally spirited English poet with a rare, agonizing disease, developed from collodion ichthyosis. When drugs offered no relief or necessitated tapering off, NATURE, she vowed (in all caps), was the only healer. Afflicted since birth, she recalled suffering greatly one day as a child, going outside and lying down on her back in the grass. When she stood up she beheld a glimmer of blue silhouetting her body that quickly dematerialized. She ran inside to tell her parents, who were watching the telly, and they told her not to worry about it. The phenomenon never recurred, but lying down next to the earth continued to soothe her. It was not enough to sit in the shade on a bench. Total physical contact was essential to receive the succor offered.

I would lie in the duff of a fern leaf in Warren, RI, were distress, mental or physical, to guide me there.

~

                                          Never a hanging tree:
but Joan of Arc was thought by her examiners to be receiving satanic messages
from a Fairy Tree, a beech, alas.

The tree was on the grounds of Bourlémont Castle, the château upon which the
villagers of Domrémy toiled for their grindstone lives. This was the Fairy Tree
L'Arbre des Dames or Le Beau Mai tree, whereupon extra-ecclesiastic celebrations
were staged.

It stood near a healing well in a grove of oaks. The tree was deemed the source of
the voices she heard. She denied all this crap.

    Joan of Arc dressed like a (demonic) guy.
    Heard (demonic) voices.
    The Fairy Tree, a (demonic) beech, was a pagan site (demonic).
    Joan heard (demonic) voices under the tree (demonic).
    The (demonic) tree was by a (demonic) healing fountain. (Demonic.)
    Joan did not believe in the (demonic) healing fountain.
    Joan had never heard the (demonic) tree speak.
    Not in the fields when the church bells rang.
    Saint Joan was a virgin.

              ~

A professor at Cornell University has been worrying about European beech
decline for decades.

He thinks the assassin is a relative of the microbe that caused the Irish potato famine. He and colleagues have identified a particular *Phytophthora*. Related to brown algae. The same genus has been identified with Sudden Oak Death in California. But a pathologist in Corvallis, OR, has determined it to be a different pathogen.

Both start with bleeding cankers in the bark.

In the Northeast approximately 40 percent have cankers.

Fewer on American than on European coppers.

The bleeding has alcohol content attracting ambrosia beetles.

Then comes the two-lined chestnut borer. It sets upon the stressed.

Wilted foliage, sign of the borer.

Collar rot and aerial bleeding cankers of beech caused by *P. cambivora* attack the fine roots; *P. cactorum* and *P. citricola* cause damping off. There is also *P. gonapodyides,* another isolated devil of a *Phytophthora.* (More *LFs.*)

Phytophthora: plant destroyer. Wherever you step in the soil.

The Europeans burn easily. Once the foliage is stripped they are subject to sunscald.

The new silvicultural concept, spurred by widespread nursery infestation, of planting groups of broadleaf trees in pure conifer forests and replacing conifer forests by broadleaved or mixed-forest trees in order to stabilize the woods against predicted climatic changes is likely to fail, according to an independent scientist in Brannenburg.

~

A cool zone 8
      is cool
A hot zone 8
      not so cool
That's an Oceanic
      yes
A Continental
      n-o

Zones 4–7. Zones 3–8. Depending on the literature. Either way, it's a generous temperate spread.

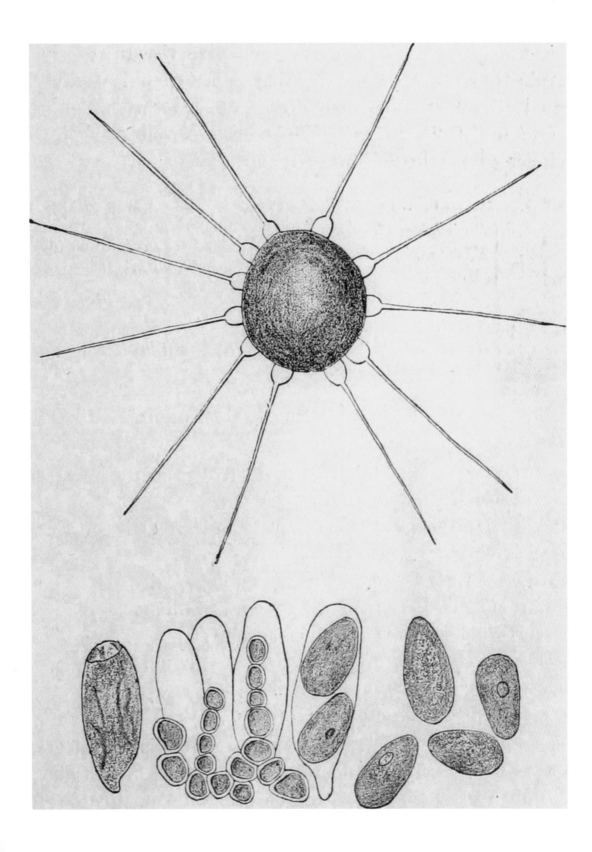

~

Ohio plains poet Merrill Gilfillan describes the nut to a T:

A quart and a half in an oval wicker basket, fresh and plump, honey yaller palomino in spots, or dun with rusty highlights (the vibrissa on the hulls), the hulls each with a tiny handle-sprig in varying stages of opening, like mussels in a pot. In hand, the fruit within peek out, elegant pairs of shiny three-sided shells a workshoe/drayhorse brown.

~

Fagus sylvatica 'Purpurea': first mentioned in a nurseryman's catalogue in America, 1820.
Their catalogue appearance noted by Arnold Arboretum's first director, botanist Charles Sprague Sargent.

Thomas Jefferson ordered purple beeches from Thomas Main's nursery in 1807. Planted them at Monticello. The first spring planting failed; so he ordered them again in the fall. One blew down in the 1950s (its replacement fell to disease in 2001), the other lived until the 1970s.

The trees must have been planted by Wormley Hughes—grandson of Elizabeth Hemings, born at Monticello—a slave, who started working there as a boy. Though he was freed by Martha Randolph, his wife and eight children were sold to a University of Virginia prof. Most were brought back together later on the plantation of Thomas Randolph, Jefferson's grandson. Among the many holes Mr. Hughes dug, one was the President's grave.

~

Tucson ca. 1981: Making myself at home in the editor of *Ironwood*'s bathroom, I picked up a local independent paper. A Mexican playwright, from Guadalajara, stated that when you talk about how beautiful a city is, you are talking about its trees. I wish I had snagged the tabloid—I wanted to know more about writers in Guadalajara, where I once visited and overall thought cars and factories had made a hellish metropolis of what had been a beautiful city. Six million and growing. Also credited for bringing us mariachi music, for which I can't express heartfelt gratitude. And tequila, for which I can.

Guadalajara
river of stones
heavenly
weather
flowering
trees
abundant

Its water source
Lake Chapala
shallow
and
drying up

Spring last:
eighteen
bodies
without heads
discovered
on an access
road
stuffed
into vans

eighteen
bodies
stuffed
into vans
no heads

On a second spring trip to Guadalajara, the frangipani were showing off.

~

Walking through a New Hampshire wood on the land of a friend, a wholehearted Manhattan expat—abrupt, bordering on gruff on the exterior, but innocent in his habit. We tramped through the dense understory. He would stop to scrub his poison ivy—of which he had an impressive case—with jewelweed. (Looking cortisone-time to me.) We passed an old soul, not falling but leaning in the direction of hitting the ground. He said when he'd had cancer he often came to this tree, and I could hug it if I wanted. Embarrassed to hug it then and there, but tentatively, I did. Who knows when an otherwise inexplicable transference of strength might strike.

I will think often of the young English poet with ichthyosis rising to her little stricken feet swathed by a blue aura.

~

The Judge was astounded when lightning struck the hickory in the Boone Co. courthouse square and the blackened tree sold for $1,000. He felt, though fully knew otherwise, that trees were commonly held property. Felt, though knew otherwise, they had no real monetary value. It would be like owning the ocean, was his thinking.

~

Gary Allen's Tramp Recipe, Beechnut Cake:

Scald and peel
the nuts,
pound them
and
mix with flour,
eggs, butter
or margarine,
one part
beechnuts
to two parts
of the other stuff.
Bake.

~

In the Southern Hemisphere there is another genus, *Nothofagus.* Charles Sprague Sargent reported that the beech forests of the mountains of southern Chile were the most beautiful he had ever seen. As I said, it is another genus of the otherworld variety.

A photograph in *Smithsonian Magazine* is of a clonally reproducing beech in Queensland, Australia. 12,000 years. Spreading north from Antarctica when the cold grew too intense for it there. The photographer shoots old living organisms. Her cutoff is 2,000 years. No merely senior-discount specimens qualify.

Photographs of Antarctic beeches are not completely believable, but an image of a forest of them resembles nothing more than mega-magnified-and-enhanced broccoli.

~

In the spring of 2009 when David Hockney returned to a familiar copse to paint the beeches and sycamores near his home, he found "a massacre." Planted a hundred years ago as a shelter for farm building and fields, they had been felled as they presented a safety issue for the nearby cottages. Planted as a windbreak. Downed as a hazard. The property now owned by a kitchen tycoon. Chop chop.

(Two Hockneys, summer & winter, had been completed before the massacre.)

Nobody asked about these trees. Nobody asks enough questions anymore. The painter rued.

I think now, says Hockney, this is my next painting of the wood. It will be very different, but the piles of wood are quite beautiful in their own right, simply because

                                        wood
                                        can't help
                                        being
                                        beautiful.

One craftsman has been turning goblets and plates and bowls on the lathe from one branch of an iconic copper beech that once stood at the Eugene O'Neill Theater Center in Waterford, CT. Carry it forward.

Artist Richard Fishman sought to save a 100-year-old elm on Brown University's campus. The architects obligingly designed the new policy institute around it. The tree was framed up and sedated. Basically rendered comatose. Survived the building, but weakened, succumbed shortly after to Dutch elm. Fishman and students filmed the felling. Secured an underused storage space for its carcass off-site. Built a woodshop around it. Every morsel of the centurial tree, down to its sawdust, was metamorphosed for functional and nonfunctional objects by the students from Brown and Rhode Island School of Design and visiting artists. Carry it forward.

Reminding me of Sierra naturalist David Lukas describing the aspen's state of being as *theoretical immortality.* An Ice Age tree, it is believed to harbor its seeds under the mother tree waiting for the next climatic change to disperse them.

Suddenly rousing an image of the Virginia camp my husband attended as a child. So did our son in turn. The matriarch of the family presiding over the camp woke to a 3-story sycamore outside her window. Fond as she still was of living, she told me she would not want to outlive that tree that she had loved all her days.

~

Long long ago they were all over Antarctica.

And America with its own genus.

The young ones need care. The old

generally prefer to be undisturbed.

Sometimes they are so tall and straight

and smooth they look like nothing

so much as columns of limestone.

~

I frequently tramped eight or ten miles through the deepest snow to keep an
appointment with a beech tree.   Thoreau

…which has so neat a bole and beautifully lichen painted, perfect in all its details, of which, excepting scattered specimens, I know but one small grove of sizable trees left in the township, supposed by some to have been planted by the pigeons that were once baited with beech nuts near by.   Ibid

Audubon's account of the passenger pigeon (*Ectopistes migratorius*) is so dramatically tied up with beech trees and with a pattern of waste to which Americans seem hell-bent, I must quote, as has been done before, at length from his *Ornithological Biography:*

In the autumn of 1813, I left my house at Henderson, on the banks of the Ohio, on my way to Louisville. In passing over the Barrens a few miles beyond Hardensburgh, I observed the pigeons flying from north-east to south-west, in greater numbers than I thought I had ever seen them before, and feeling an inclination to count the flocks that might pass within the reach of my eye in one hour, I dismounted, seated myself on an eminence, and began to mark with my pencil, making a dot for every flock that passed. In a short time finding the task which I had undertaken impracticable, as the birds poured in in countless multitudes, I rose, and counting the dots then put down, found that 163 had been made in twenty-one minutes. I travelled on, and still met more the farther I proceeded. The air was literally filled with Pigeons; the light of noon-day was obscured as by an eclipse; the dung fell in spots, not unlike melting flakes of snow; and the continued buzz of wings had a tendency to lull my senses to repose....

Before sunset I reached Louisville, distant from Hardensburgh fifty-five miles. The Pigeons were still passing in undiminished numbers, and continued to do so for three days in succession. The people were all in arms. The banks of the Ohio were crowded with men and boys, incessantly shooting at the pilgrims, which there flew lower as they passed the river. Multitudes were thus destroyed. For a week or more, the population fed on no other flesh than that of Pigeons, and talked of nothing but Pigeons....

Let us now, kind reader,
inspect their place of nightly rendezvous. One of these curious roosting-places, on the
banks of the Green River in Kentucky, I repeatedly visited. It was, as is always the
case, in a portion of the forest where the trees were of great magnitude,
and where there was little underwood....

Few Pigeons
were then to be seen, but a great number of persons, with horses and wagons,
guns and ammunition, had already established encampments on the borders.
Two farmers from the vicinity of Russelsville, distant more than a hundred miles,
had driven upwards of three hundred hogs to be fattened on the pigeons which
were to be slaughtered. Here and there the people employed in plucking and salting
what had already been procured, were seen sitting in the midst of large piles of these
birds. The dung lay several inches deep, covering the whole extent of the roosting-
place, like a bed of snow. Many trees two feet in diameter, I observed, were broken
off at no great distance from the ground; and the branches of many of the largest and
tallest had given way, as if the forest had been swept by a tornado. Every thing proved
to me that the number of birds resorting to this part of the forest must be immense
beyond conception. As the period of their arrival approached, their foes anxiously
prepared to receive them. Some were furnished with iron-pots containing sulphur,
others with torches of pine-knots, many with poles, and the rest with guns. The sun
was lost to our view, yet not a Pigeon had arrived. Every thing was ready, and all eyes
were gazing on the clear sky, which appeared in glimpses amidst the tall trees.
Suddenly there burst forth a general cry of "Here they come!"

Audubon painted his *Passenger Pigeon,* a pair, in Kentucky, when a young husband. On a beech bough. With two marcescent leaves. Fall. When the mast is ripe. One of the most unstintingly tender male/female pictures ever drawn. Mind, he shot the pigeons painted there.

The noise which they made, though yet distant, reminded me of a hard gale at sea, passing through the rigging of a close-reefed vessel. As the birds arrived and passed over me, I felt a current of air that surprised me. Thousands were soon knocked down by the pole-men. The birds continued to pour in.

The fires were lighted, and a magnificent, as well as wonderful and almost terrifying, sight presented itself. The Pigeons, arriving by thousands, alighted everywhere, one above another, until solid masses as large as hogsheads were formed on the branches all round. Here and there the perches gave way under the weight with a crash, and, falling to the ground, destroyed hundreds of the birds beneath, forcing down the dense groups with which every stick was loaded. It was a scene of uproar and confusion. I found it quite useless to speak, or even to shout to those persons who were nearest to me. Even the reports of the guns were seldom heard, and I was made aware of the firing only by seeing the shooters reloading....

The Pigeons were constantly coming, and it was past midnight before I perceived a decrease in the number of those that arrived. The uproar continued the whole night....

PLATE LXII.

Passenger Pigeon.
COLUMBA MIGRATORIA, Linn.
Male 1. Female 2.

The howlings of the wolves
now reached our ears, and the foxes, lynxes, cougars, bears, raccoons, opossums
and pole-cats were seen sneaking off, whilst eagles and hawks of different species, accompanied
by a crowd of vultures, came to supplant them, and enjoy their share of the spoil.

It was then that the authors of all this devastation
began their entry amongst the dead, the dying, and the mangled. The pigeons
were picked up and piled in heaps, until each had as many as he could possibly
dispose of, when the hogs were let loose to feed on the remainder.

Persons unacquainted with these birds
might naturally conclude that such dreadful havock would soon put an end to the species.
But I have satisfied myself, by long observation, that nothing but the gradual diminution
of our forests can accomplish their decrease, as they not unfrequently quadruple their
numbers yearly, and always at least double it.

The passenger pigeon laid one egg a year.

They constituted metropolises of their laying grounds.

They fed their hatchlings crop milk for several days;
then, *Sayōnara* baby.

The last actual known one in the wild was shot by a 14-year-old boy in 1900.

The last known passenger pigeon in captivity was Martha. She died in the Cincinnati Zoo, was donated to the Smithsonian, stuffed, mounted, and displayed with the inscription: MARTHA: Last of her species, died at 1 p.m., 1 September 1914, age 29, in the Cincinnati Zoological Garden. EXTINCT.

(Martha's centennial year she was brought out of the safe for her public.)

There is an unearthly portrayal of a slaughtering by blinding torchlight by Jean-François Millet (better recognized for peasants praying in a field over their mean potato yield). Frantic *Bird's-Nesters* hangs at the Philadelphia Museum of Art.

~

Pure woods of beech I think you will not find.

Infinis, a wind-farm developer, aims to rip out century-old beech trees lining a road near Chester, Scotland. The planned "24,000 construction traffic movements" and large tree removal, by their determination, will have negligible environmental impact. No developer has been recorded to ever say otherwise. Is it possible developers have actually been hurtled here from another yet more myopically inhabited orb?

Beeches are not famous for surviving bulldozer blight.

The country's second-biggest sweet gum was cut down in Alexandria, VA, for an office development. To survive, the gum tree needed a 50-foot radius. Unacceptable, said the developers—that would be 10 surface parking spaces and 15 garage spaces. Three beeches were planted after its removal. Wonder, how are they faring?

The beech is invariably listed as a park tree not a parking lot tree.

As I said, beech and oak and chestnut belong to the same large, competitive family.

The aforementioned beeches of Oradell were scheduled to bear silent, unsworn witness to Benedict Arnold being traded there for a British soldier. That didn't happen.

~

Trees live long lives. Anything can happen. Come ice or wind or fire, or human disturbance, the effects are broad and dragged out.

Out of angiosperms, oak, beech, elms, etcetera, etcetera, etcetera. 120 million years ago.

Mast from *F. grandifolia* may be the most important food source for *Ursus americana,* the American black bear. It would take a lot of nuts to stuff a hungry bear. Esp way up north where the woods are dominated by spruce.

Did you know that the leaf of *F. grandifolia* produces the most nitrogen of all the trees in North America.

As a nitrogen sink in the soil, however, its mortality rate impacts the nitrogen cycle.

Under their abundant canopy, scant sky.

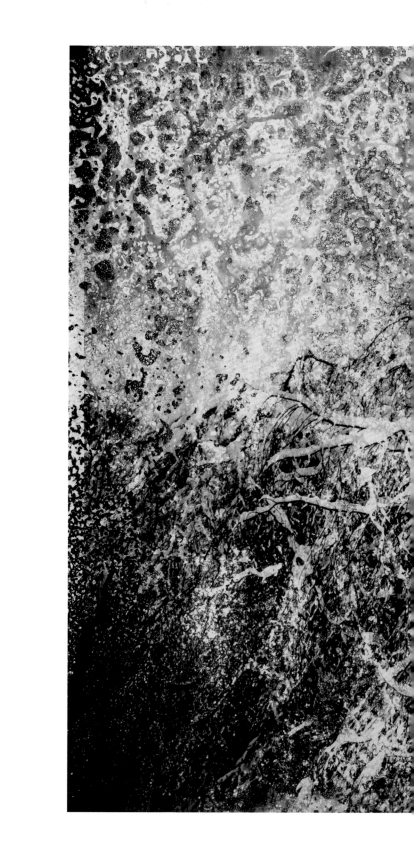

~

There is a copper in Drownville, West Barrington, RI, a couple or three miles from our house. Oooolala. I took my father, an *Arkansawyer ozarkensis,* to see it. The owner happened to be walking his property. He and Dad had a brief exchange (friendly by New England standards) about his handsome tree. My father was not gregarious, not by a stretch, nor was he intimidated by the unfamiliar. And was he ever delighted by the sight of that splendiferous example.

When those owners sold the house they moved into a newly built house behind it, with purposeful sightlines to the tree. It was in the contract that the tree could not be cut while they lived there. They have since moved elsewhere. The tree stayed put but could use some TLC. Or a lot. The trunk is cankerous and bleeding. You might still fall off your bike in goosenecking-wonder, if, pedaling past, you happen to gander in its direction.

~

Newport is RI's exhibition space for European beech trees.

As a man at my university messaged—himself an avid gardener—*Fagus sylvatica* is *de rigueur* at the Newport "cottages," over 200 of which were built in the last decades of the 19th century. When one cottage burned, and they frequently did, a more ginormous and sumptuous one had to be built in its place.

Newporters preferred their gardeners to be Scots; butlers, English, esp of the snooty variety (sporting a semipermanent expression of the faint smell of shit on the upper lip); maids, Swedish. (Uncommonly a native son would make the head-gardener cut. Mrs. Cornelius Vanderbilt at The Breakers was served for almost 60 years by a local, William Murphy, outliving both the Mister and the Missus, as well as restoring the grounds after the hurricane devastation of 1938.)

Newport's Salve Regina University maintains a weeping beech that is knees-to-the-ground commanding. The Tree of the Year is a recently instituted tradition in the city aiming for arboretum status, but the beeches are hard to surpass. The copper (*F. sylvatica* 'Cuprea') on Touro (home of the country's oldest synagogue), the fern leaf (*F. sylvatica* 'Asplenifolia') at Salve Regina, and a fern leaf at Fort Adams were last year's winners. We are still waiting for this year's results. The trees appear disinterested. They are just trying to get by.

The Redwood Library and Athenaeum in Newport, RI (founded 1747), the country's oldest lending library, holds claim to the oldest fern leaf in the country (1835), and "one of the choicest sylvan objects that belong to our climate." L.W. Russell, Principal, Bridgham Grammar School, Providence, 1897. First there were three. The one in the middle, when slated for felling, was saved by Doris Duke and moved to her Newport mansion, Rough Point. I have not learned what happened to the third, but I did discover that Ms. Duke's pet camels waited out Hurricane Bob in the solarium.

The Newport *Civic League Bulletin* of July 1910 asserts that the library's tree had been threatened by a steamroller, but was preserved by "its vigilant guardian." City parks were deemed underkept, and more rubbish barrels needed for the "peanut-eating population."

When the British were still fighting for their hold on the Colonies they cut as many of Newport's trees as they had ax and time to down, a variant on burn the houses…

As the grand beeches of Newport are now giving way, ingenious afterlives are made of their remnants.

The current owner of Bellevue House, a Colonial Revival mansion, hired carver Justin Gordon to create smartly dressed monkeys with spyglasses from the top of his standing dead beech trunks. The house was designed by Ogden Codman Jr. for his cousin Martha, who married a Russian tenor three decades her junior. Codman also wrote *The Decoration of Houses* with Edith Wharton and designed her Newport summer house, Land's End. Bellevue was subsequently owned by a Ziegfeld Girl, and so on, before passing into the hands of Ronald Lee Fleming, an urban planner and preservationist. His 3-day 70th birthday in Newport featured a New Orleans jazz funeral parade; first liners were the invitees. I wasn't among them, but am doubtful of a second line, and contrary to tradition, a living body was being celebrated. In 2013 Newport declared July 11 in his honor, a water ballet among the features. All of this seemingly tame by New Orleans standards, where parties and parades are taken to pink-giraffe extremes.

(Wharton's Land's End was later bought by Oatsie Charles, granddaughter of a Confederate commander who went on to become Alabama governor, herself the widow of Thomas Leiter, heir to Marshall Field stores. Nonagenarian Oatsie reigns on, in the gardener's house, The Whim.)

The Merrillton cottage, an Italianate villa, built in 1853 by Samuel Powel; bought by a Rev. George Merrill, married to Pauline, a sister-in-law of John Nicholas Brown; sold to Georgia-born singer Jane Pickens; inherited by her daughter, Marcella Clark McCormack; sold to Peter de Savary in 2012, British exporter, oil, shipping, imports, and real estate entrepreneur; has been sold again this year to Peter Lindsay Jenkins, pharmaceutical magnate. It was Mr. de Savary, I believe, who had the center cored out of a dead beech and another grown tree, of a different species, planted within its hollow. Go figure. Merrillton's "famous" tree is a European hornbeam.

With an introduction from Chris Fletcher of Bartlett Tree Experts, George and Nannette Herrick allowed me to watch their best-loved beech be brought to the ground. Mrs. Herrick said her grandson was going to be so mad when he came to town to find his favorite climber gone. Mrs. Herrick wanted the tree cut to the grass. She did not want the stump to linger as a reminder.

The Herricks directed me to an old-growth forest on former Vanderbilt land, just off Aquidneck Island in Portsmouth, RI. Condo developers had hired an Oregon logger, Matthew Largess to take out 20 acres of beech. He had been involved in logging in the eighties when dynamite was used to blow out the holes under 1,500-year-old Sitka spruce, with Japanese logging ships, sawmills on deck, idling offshore. Lights were used to keep operations going 24/7 knowing they could be shut down at any moment. Largess had his eureka flash in Rhode Island, realizing the trees he was hired to raze were old growth, calling in a scientist to verify their age instead of commencing to clear-cut. In 2000 the land named Oakland Forest was turned over to the Aquidneck Island Land Trust, which had obtained the necessary funds through donations to purchase the property from the developers. And Logger Largess became a caretaker of venerable trees. He said it was like an alcoholic becoming sober, an atheist getting religion: Logger → Largess.

Although it is the mansions that buses roll oglers into Newport for, the city's aristocratic beech trees are synonymous with the Gilded Age. Without them many of the houses would reveal themselves as gaudy mausoleums. White elephants, in the mind of Henry James, who spent much of his teens there.

When the tobacco and electric power king James Buchanan Duke died in his own white elephant in New York City, he left his Newport mansion and most of his fortune to his 12-year-old daughter, Doris.

The authorship of *The Gilded Age: A Tale of Today* is shared by Charles Dudley Warner and Mark Twain. But the term *Gilded Age* was probably Twain's. He had a knack for tagging.

No palace on Newport's Bellevue Avenue would be properly palatial without European beeches: esp the common, the copper, and the weeper. Now at a minimum 120 years old they are calling it quits left and right.

Some say they are just aging out. But that's not truly old for these hardy trees; though they are not native here, it is favored clime, favored earth.

One obvious problem is having planted so many trees during the same period.

One local arborist suggests that their early demise might be attributed to their being specimen trees, generally grafted and often standing in full sun.

Penelope Creeley, a fine gardener, suggests that if they have been over-fertilized, they could peak and poop out as she has seen many a plant do, but demurs on tree expertise.

A century earlier it was the Europeans collecting American specimens. They were gaga for our trees. Kindly John Bartram was most obliging in sending seedlings to a Londoner "brother of the spade." The Revolutionary War briefly interrupted this exchange. And though they had shortages, England held off for a period, due to rancor over the outcome.

France however came agathering. The seeds François André Michaux collected grew over a quarter of a million trees in France. His 3-vol *North American Sylva* was the first of its kind regarding trees east of the Mississippi River. John Perlin's *A Forest Journey* reports that Michaux's father's collection had previously been catalogued in books on the oaks and the flora of America and exploited by the noblemen who distributed seeds among themselves intended for his country's woodland.

In the Gilded Age, anything and everything European was the bee's knees.

The Breakers, Chateau-sur-Mer, The Elms, Kingscote, Marble House, Rosecliff are all graced with beech trees, as is Salve Regina University, as is the Redwood Library with its fern-leaved brought over in a bottle by a young girl on a ship, goes the oft-told story. Jefferson and Washington both visited the Grecian-temple-inspired library. British officers took it over during their occupation. Boots up on the reading tables.

Others say soil compaction should shoulder the blame. So much traffic over the years, foot and motor. Others say canker, fungus, and insect.

Compacted soil is extra-detrimental to these trees. People are given to parking their cars in the shade under the trees, running their mowers over the roots, holding secret (demonic) meetings around the trunk, and so forth.

The artist's conk (*Ganoderma applanatum*) and the tinder fungus (*Fomes fomentarius*) are two predators of the American beech. The fruiting body of the latter, which can live for more than 70 years, is a record holder for decaying fungi. (*LFs.*)

For a certain cast and age of us, it is not the supersized cottages or the trees or the now-for-sale America's Cup that put Newport on the map, but its being where Dylan went electric in 1965.

There is, I am told, a certain class of ladies in Newport who like to start drinking before noon. If I lived there, I'd probably long to join in. Wrong class, wrong time of day, and it's not a joiner's prerogative.

But come winter, come winter, there is no place I would prefer to wander in. Come summer it is high on the list of places my sort tend to avoid.

There are lesions. Then comes a red resin.

Soil borne. *Phytophthora citricola.* A musical appellation. A pity.

Entry at the root collars.

Less common on the American.

Most common on the European coppers.

The same fungicide is used to treat trees suffering from Sudden Oak Death.

Heart rot. Another fungus, such as *Fistulina hepatica,* as the name indicates, rots the wood at the heart. Mushrooms may signal heart rot. The wound was there first. The spores enter the wounds and germinate and, nibble by nibble, ingest the heartwood.

A tea is used to renew the roots.

The best compost costs $44 per cubic yard.

The AirSpade® is a handheld tool that produces a stream of supersonic air to break up compacted soil.

Under the drip line, mulch with its own leaves.

The False Blusher (panther cap) is symbiotic at the level of the roots. *Cuidado:* psychedelic but poisonous (potentially lethal) 'shroom.

At least the Judas's Ear fungus is edible. Along with the oyster mushroom.

Then there's the *Hebeloma sinapizans* forming a fairy ring at the drip line. Makes for a bitter poison pie.

A FAIRY RING

The big weeper at The Elms is oozing.

The Elms served as the summer home of the coal magnate Edward Julius Berwind and wife. Designed after the 18th-century Château d'Asnières. The specimen trees planted between 1907 and 1914. The carriage house was converted to a garage when the automobile came into being, and the coachman became the driver, but like Gertrude Stein, he did not learn to back up. In his case a turntable was installed to bring the car around. The elms themselves died of Dutch elm disease. The mansion maintained a staff of 40 during season. Rather, a staff of 40 maintained the mansion and its occupants. The servants were kept ingeniously out of sight when not directly waiting on family and guests.

Visiting The Elms' weeper with arborist Chris Fletcher, I was shown how to get a panorama of the tree in its amplitude. The arborist had long lost count of how many times he had taken his/her picture. Nor did he/she ever tire of being photographed.

~

Scale is one guilty insect. Then comes the nectria canker. Caused by the fungi *N. cinnabarina* and *N. galligena*. It develops a slow-growing, vagina-shaped area on the bark. Not usually fatal, but a stunter.

Crush the vile grubs of the weevil, beech leaf-miner. An evil weevil aka flea weevil you have to pick off and squish or set fire to. Feeds on the leaves, yet the trees often survive their noshing.

Beech bark aphid, *Fagiphagus imbricator,* beech eater aka *Little Fuckers.*

The saddled prominent and gypsy moths and the Bruce spanworm have been among its defoliators. (Likewise *LFs.*)

The beech bark scale coupled with the fungus causes BBD, beech bark disease, thought to have entered the continent by way of Europe through Nova Scotia. First found in Europe in 1840. In Nova Scotia in 1920. By the decade's end, in Massachusetts.

The scale is a female-only population.

The felted beech coccus (*Cryptococcus fagisuga*) enters the bark. Then the fungus (*Nectria coccinea*) infects the tree. The bigger the tree the more susceptible.

The whitefly elicits a lengthy list of treatments: soapy water, strong hose, earthworm castings, spiderwebs, vacuuming, orange oil, motor oil, assassin bugs, water-soaked-and-diluted cigar spray, worm juice tea, ladybugs… then there is the rugose spiraling whitefly aka gumbo limbo spiraling whitefly in the company of over 1,550 whitefly species having been identified. And counting.

When a tree trunk is girdled by insect or canker expansion it exposes the cambium and the tree dies.

(The cambium grows with the tree, sideways.)

The shoestring fungus *Armillaria* is a girdler.

The light that penetrates those transparent leaves pleases.

Damping off (another pathogenic assault) aborts the seedlings or
creates weaklings.

Burls, those tumorish growths you sometimes see on the trunks, are purported to wall off the growth of disease. The tree however could continue to rot from within.

Beech burls are being removed illegally in Massachusetts. Burl is keenly coveted by furniture makers.

Same goes for the redwood burls in the West. Poachers chainsawing the Coast redwoods (*Sequoia sempervirens*) in the dead of night in the public parks covering too much area to police.

Removing a burl from the trunk can be fatal to the tree.

These trees, according to one specialist, owe far more of their regeneration to burls than seedlings. A Bolinas arborist says that's an oversimplification, but the burls do sprout, and the genetic code to the parent tree is stored therein.

Beech can reproduce by root suckers.

The European doesn't sprout as much from the base of the trunk.

~

Monoecious. From Greek *monos* (single) + *oikos* (house). Male and female flowers on the same tree. That simplifies one thing.

(Male flowers, yellow; female flowers, green.)

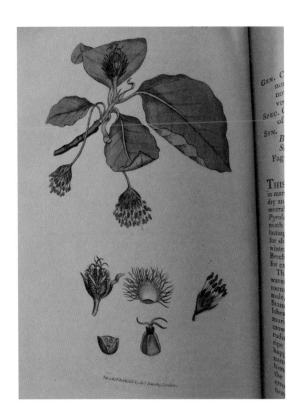

We had a young holly planted recently, and the nursery assured me contact would be made with the holly on the other side of the house bordering the burial ground. Whether they pair up or not, as much as I try not to anthropomorphize, even given that a solitary tree in a field takes my breath, I do not like to think of a tree being the only one of its kind for miles around.

~

Newport's Preservation Society arborist grows European beeches grafted to rootstock from the American beech.

Many anatomists decline to draw a hard line between the Europeans and the Americans. But Gordon Saltar's discovery of the particular presence of tandem rays and crystals in an American variety apparently confirms they are a different species.

Because some of the plants growing around the beech trunks (such as *Luzula luzuloides*) are different than those around other trees in a mixed forest, researchers argue for the designation of a discrete ecological zone.

Between the copper ('Cuprea') and the purple ('Purpurea') is a graded journey of cloudy distinctions.

Furthermore: To keep a clear distinction between native and nonnative species requires nearly geologic memory. But humans, like most species, don't live in the past, where the distinction originates.   Verlyn Klinkenborg

Speaking of point of origin, from the big window in Petaluma I can see: eucalyptus (Australia), coast redwood (native), spruce (Australia), live oak (native), bottlebrush (Australia), California walnut, olive (Mediterranean, Asia, Africa), fan palm (Mexico, not a true tree; the seeds of which are said to germinate best from coyote dung), a pepper tree and an avocado on the corner (Peru; Mexico and Central America), an Atlas cedar (Algeria), and five more evergreens I can't identify even with books and Leafsnap app; also a Southern magnolia, a fig (Mideast and Asia), persimmon (China) now bare of leaves and loaded with glossy yellow-orange balls I thought, on first sighting, were ornaments. Yesterday I saw a dollhouse-sized tree decked out with full-sized pomegranates (Iran to Indian Himalayas), and next to my favorite secondhand store, a small tree redolent with lemons (Asia). And without moving an inch, an intelligent crow being mobbed by a single violet-green swallow. Go, Mom.

Standing on the deck with a delivery man. He says that if you just get rid of that pine you'll have a great view of the football field. You mean that *Sequoia sempervirens*. (#$@&%*!.)

~

A London mathematician professes that the jay does not disperse the beech, but prefers the oak. He further claims that the most beautiful tree in the world is the eucalyptus. Inarguably beautiful, but they are some kind of trashy damn tree. Picking up after one is an unending task, recommended if you do not want to be thigh-high in their oily, volatile sheaths of bark and leaf.

Fueled by the Diablo winds, the Oakland hills firestorm of 1991 implicated these Tasmanian blue gums. Twenty-five lives and 4,000 dwellings, neighbors, neighborhoods, gardens, clothes, keepsakes, tools, toys and libraries, vehicles and appliances and exploding trees…

Maxine Hong Kingston picked up the white ash block of the manuscript of *The Fourth Book of Peace* in the footprint of her former home. It would be 14 years before *The Fifth Book of Peace* was released in its place with assistance from traumatized war veterans with whom she worked during those years:

fire   paper   ash   earth

(The beech is fire resistant. Does not mean it will not burn.)

One naturalist calls the eucalypts naturalized citizens. And by registry
definition a tree is naturalized once it has become common and has established
itself as though wild.

These unruly brides of disquietude are here now. Leave them be. Don't coppice.
Pick up their litter. Else import the fungus that helps them rot. Else bring on the
koalas and greater gliders.

In the predawn fog, we were driven to the airport by the lead singer for a Cream
tribute band, Ultimate Cream. He told us he used to have a business selling
eucalyptus flea collars. (Did pretty well for a while.)

Funny
how
trees
succor
us.

All the foregone Western divagations, soon to be supplanted with a Rhode Island view of oak, cedar, holly, pine, spruce, arborvitae, and *Fagus sylvatica.* There is no beech in our New England yard, but a block over I often mosey past a solid specimen to make sure he/she is staying healthy.

~

A field book author calls the beeches time travelers.

Beeches are also called selfish and ambitious.

Beeches are called tolerant and knowledgeable of history.

They are said to be gentle critics.

It is reckoned they are determined to keep fit.

Beechnut is 32 percent PUFA (polyunsaturated fatty acid).

Chemically unstable. No cook with.

~

Home in Illinois, Lincoln liked to read under a beech. Lincoln liked to read period. For all we know he may have liked to look at dirty flip books under the ample canopy of a solitary beech.

Though Lincoln was known to have enjoyed reading under a beech, it is apparently not true that he and his son Tad played and read under a copper beech at the cottage on the grounds of the Soldiers' Home. This is where Lincoln drafted the Emancipation Proclamation, and the kids could play mumble-the-whatever-the-hell-it-is-peg. This is where he rode Old Bob, grey shawl over his own grey shoulders, and though usually accompanied by a cavalry detail, did once have his high hat shot through. The tree, real enough, was probably not big enough at the time to provide shade for the idle, bookish type.

A copper beech is planted in front of his seated statue in Louisville, where with bronze book balanced on his knee, pried open by a bronze finger, he watches the Ohio roll on, where he first saw slaves unloaded, and was put wise to his revulsion toward the peculiar institution.

They are very beautiful, firm, and perfect leaves, unspotted and not eaten by insects, of a handsome, clear leather-color, like a book bound in calf. Crisp and elastic.   Thoreau

There is a Corot of a woman lying down reading in a beech grove. Really the painting is of the trees. She just happens to be in the lower-left corner, barefoot, loose-tressed, corseted. From here, the pages that absorb the woman are just gobbledygook.

Greek proverb: A civilization flourishes when people plant trees under which they will never sit—there may be more than one possible translation of that one.

African proverb: Roots do not know what a leaf has in mind.

Everytime the tree works the leaves dream.   Frank Stanford

That mono-focal experience of the *bok* is the heart and soul of what it means to read.

FYI: *Fagus sylvatica* is the most mentioned tree in Danish poetry.

FYI: The 16th president was shot in his fine Brooks Brothers suit.

~

Lightning is a quick nitrate fixer.

Oil of the beech may reduce its ability to conduct electricity.

You may have heard that lightning will not strike a beech tree. Don't fall for that one. This bit of lore is blamed on the Indians; another count on which it has been misnomered an Indian tree. Several sizzled persons have been found seated against its bole.

~

Passing the severed remains of a eucalyptus grove on South Petaluma Blvd, chopped down in the dead of night by the state agency Caltrans in preparation for altering the interchange. They were felled in January since in the spring they are the nesting grounds of egrets and herons and then come under the protection of the feds.

This stretch of land is owned by Dutra, which intends to build a big asphalt plant at Haystack Landing. They have secured 38 acres. Opposite the bird sanctuary. A moment of silence for the lost rookery. A future of pavement without which, Dutra reminds us, our kids will have no playgrounds on which to fall from their swings.

Afterword: Dutra has cleared the California State Court of Appeals.

Since when and why are playgrounds paved. Is the dirt under the swing set contaminated. Does a dirt fall hurt worse than a blacktop fall.

The eucs (the predominant one in Northern California being Tasmanian blue gum or *Eucalyptus globulus*) are embattled. Described as hyperactive, they are nonnative, invasive, and "generally disagreeable," say many. They do shed a lot, and their aromatic oils *are* susceptible to burning. They are christened dirty trees, trash, mongrels, and widow makers. Someone says their seeds are like walking on ball bearings. That their beauty is "cold and otherworldly." They get awful press. Humans aren't native either, claim some of their defenders. One dis goes, Living next to one is like living next to a fireworks factory staffed by chain-smokers.

They provide shade, windbreak, comeliness. They have thrived. They cannot just up and move back to Australia. What if koalas were brought in to curtail the shedding. Who could resist a koala. A group committed to the trees' protection uses the acronym POET (Preserve Our Eucalyptus Trees). The Euc Wars have been going on since the turn of the century and are much more involved than I can represent as a newcomer.

(European [common] beeches are obviously not native, and sadly are noninvasive. Keep in mind, *escapes are to be expected*.)

Judson Dynamite & Powder Company started planting the eucalypts in the Oakland hills in the 1880s to muffle the sound of dynamite and conceal the hideous sites caused by the blasts. Then they were planted on a grander order for timber, real estate development, and to control fires. None of the latter proved to be sound thinking. The latter latter in particular.

~

Warmer winters aren't good for beeches.

Warmer winters are upon us. (Polar vortex notwithstanding.)

In Maine the beeches soldier on in spite of the bark-feeding scale whose populations explode with the warmer winters, but they don't produce much mast for the bears.

Photographs show the Maine bears leaving puncture marks going up the trees, and parallel marks coming down in an effort to put the hard brakes on their weight.

~

A couple noticed a problem with their beeches on their land in Harbor Springs, MI, two years ago:

We'll be in bed sometimes, and we'll just hear: Whooomp!

Jojoba oil is used for aphids. If it comes to that. Replaced sperm oil from whales and is used against mildew. Being used copiously in fact. As whale sperm once was.

There is always picking them off one by one.

Parasitic wasps attack aphids.

As do ladybugs, the one bug nobody can deny. A ladybug will devour thousands of aphids in its itsy busy bitsy life.

(Keep refrigerated until use.)

There is a patient arborist named Robert Heyd in Michigan's Upper Peninsula removing limbs from healthy trees to graft in a lab. The seeds from these stand a much better chance of being disease-resistant. The goal is to then plant the healthy offspring in the wild until the numbers support their crossing with other disease-free trees, creating a viable population.

Long after the arborist and company are chewing root hairs themselves, there is hope of a comeback.

~

Beeches of Muskoka [Ontario] *Are Set to Vanish:* 350,000 hectares of forest, about 15 percent are American beech. A hectare is 2.471 acres. (Not a convenient measure here in the US. I hesitate to even say the word aloud, *hectare.* Much less, 350,000 of them.)

Most of the diseased trees in Michigan are in the Upper Peninsula and northwest Lower Peninsula. The diseased will have to be removed.

The beeches at Whitefish Dunes are now part of a timber operation. The scale they forecast would not reach them from Michigan's Upper Peninsula for a decade, hit the following year.

Something to ponder from three Canadian researchers: the cutting down of infected trees for disease control has resulted in higher numbers of beech saplings in the forest, which has an adverse effect on maple seedling survival, and results in stands of genetically susceptible American beech trees.

Mind the gap.   Beeches will fill in, but not necessarily with their strongest.

Once the scale (*C. fagisuga*) then the fungus (*Neonectria faginata* and *Neonectria ditissima*) do their dirty work, the girdling of the tree chokes off its nutrients. (*LFs.*)

Once phloem is gone, leaves can't move the sugar.

The harder they come, the harder they fall, one and all

Xylem tissue, as we know, moves the water. Phloem is the other transporter, esp of sugar. Even I remember, a dropper of seventh-grade science.

Xylem carries the water up the length of the plant, to the top of the sequoia whereas a suction pump can raise water only 10 meters. Dig this: the sequoia can raise water 100 meters. Though fog absorbed by the leaves is a major factor in its survival. Solomon the excellent plumber keeps telling me water works in strange ways.

With drought, air bubbles develop in the tubes of the xylem, obstructing the water's flow.

When it rains you get *stemflow.*

Sugar gets the tree through the winter and helps it flower and produce a full head of leaves.

When essential minerals are lacking, this is the *limiting factor.*

Drought, compacting, and fine root hairs combined, spell death. The tree cannot pick up enough water or fertilizer or store carbohydrates for wintering.

Roots glean essential minerals from the soil, esp phosphorous.

You've got three types of roots—large woody roots at base that hold the tree upright; long, slender woody roots that transport materials back to the stem; and absorbing roots that take up essential elements and water.

Roots are fibrous and feed close to the surface.

~

Kensington Gardens and Hyde Park, these are fantastic city green spaces; being Royal Parks, public use depends upon the grace of the Crown.

Elgin Garden was the first public botanical garden in America (1801), but it was so expensive to operate, founder David Hosack sold it to the state at a big loss 9 years later. The state proceeded to neglect the land; then deeded it (as a sop) to Columbia University in 1814, which in turn leased the site to John D. Rockefeller Jr. for the development of Rockefeller Center, rendering the abandoned garden the university's cash cow.

Barrington, RI, an old suburb by US standards (founded in the 17th century), boasted a rosarian of the first order who went to the town to see whether he could get a tax write-off by opening his grounds to the public (which he often graciously did on an informal basis). The town declined outright. The rosarian was priced out of his land and sold it off in parcels. In the last 10 years, the roses have been reduced to perhaps three bushes. Now the land is full of numbingly look-alike residences, yielding their share of taxes, but it doesn't take a wizard to surmise more gains from a garden of real consequence. The greatest green space left in the community is dedicated to the country club's groomed, rolling course.

In Providence, there are a number of small parks, with various lovely trees, and virtually no one visiting them. Fine for drug deals by night. Empty benches by day. They are one frame off, location-wise, not positioned where people walk or cycle or can park a vehicle. Plus, the habit of the small urban park has not established itself to wipe off the bird shit and sit with fresh baguette and wedge of cheese. To read. To amble. To visit. To stroke the chin over a cement board of hand-carved chess pieces. To watch a fan-shaped leaf drift to the grass.

The site where Roger Williams was purportedly greeted by the Narragansett sachem—"What cheer, Netop"—is such a park. Once on the river, now some rods inland due to fill and construction. Marked by a nondescript monolith from which the bronze tablets have been stolen, and a lone row of ginkgoes that drop their leaves on cue, en masse, late fall. The park has been restored to its former nongrandeur, but its usage still seems to be: vacant by day, drug deals by night. I don't know what it needs—a sturdy set of swings, day lilies, a fountain, and maybe an inviting beech tree. The slope looks right, and the interior is open for the kind of space a specimen tree aspires.

~

A tree can only take so many insults. Esp when geriatric and distressed.

Commonly a tree dies of hunger or thirst. As did my mother, as a result of Alzheimer's.

~

The low swooping branches may be there to protect its sensitive cambium.
        Where the cells multiply.

                The low branches that take root are known as *outriggers.*

It is the cambium that produces the tissue wood. Between the phloem and xylem.

Ross is the rough outer bark; also a transitive verb, to remove the bark.

        Female flowers are paired. The flower is without petal.

~

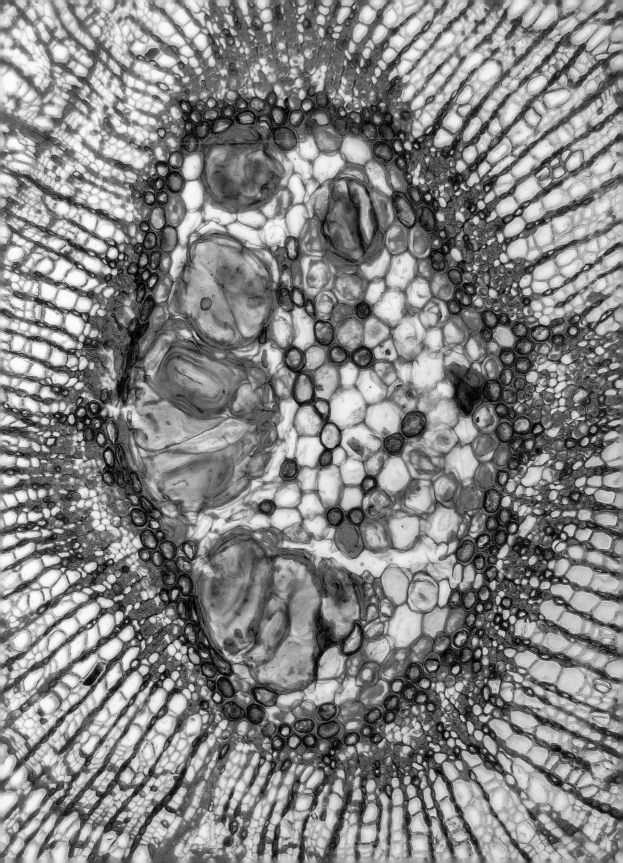

EVERY LIVING THING COMPETES:

Water for oxygen, oxygen for water, oxygen and water for pore space in the soil.

If New York is
our nerve center for competition
Los Angeles is the slacker
Then there are the Ozarks of Arkansas
birthplace of Walmart
(4,000 stores in the US, 2,000 in Mexico alone)
The triumph was Teotihuacan
City of the Gods
built in the shadow of the Pyramid
of the Moon & the Pyramid of the Sun,
a Supercenter,
the Temple of Sam
in the middle of Elda Pineda's alfalfa field
backed by bribes to
change the zoning
Competition the Walmart way
Don't blame it on the Mexicanos
No arruinar las ruinas
was the cry in the *calles*
Where have all the one-person stalls
and peppertrees
(*Schinus molle*) of the wide valley gone
ask the Sons of Sam

~

Once beeches reach 40 years of age, they begin to produce large quantities of nuts that are eaten by more than 40 species of birds and mammals.

That's 30 years to maturity for the European (*F. sylvatica*), 40+ for the American (*F. grandifolia*). This qualifies the Americans as late starters, a condition with which many of us may identify.

Beech and oak in Britain are *normally* around 60 years old before they flower, the number affected by growing conditions—shade being primary.

The American beech favors shade. As do the Europeans.

Who doesn't, favors melanoma.

The beech is adept at intercepting light in the understory.

$\sim$

According to the law of succession, beeches appear in the final stage—this is when the shade trees dominate the canopy. Dominate the understory. Domination is the name of the game.

Occur in pure stands. Occur with sugar maple.

Occur with yellow birch and eastern hemlock.

In the South may occur with magnolia. That would be a sight, an old-time beauty pageant, but apparently they are on view on the Ozark Highlands Trail.

Coppers occur in the wild from a genetic mutation.

Even from seed a copper will often produce a green tree.

Occur with hornbeam. Also named horse beech, blue beech, white beech, Hurst beech. Not a beech. An extra-hard wood. Makes for good chopping blocks and gun butts.

Leaf pigments are water soluble. The hue depends upon the pH levels.

A cut-leaf can have a branch or so of standard-issue beech design.

~

Most of American chestnuts (*Castanea dentata*) were lost to a fungus from imported Asian chestnuts. First noticed in the Bronx Zoo in 1904. The Asian trees came with a strong resistance, but the American trees fell on a massive scale (3 billion + or −) to chestnut blight. This left the oaks and beeches to provide the mast upon which so much animal life depends. Unlike oaks and beeches, the American chestnuts produced meganuts annually and began producing at an early age. The largest group of planted survivors is in Oregon. Many an Appalachian string instrument was made from its wood. There are "old soldiers" in the wild, and there are bands of professionals and volunteers dedicated to their restoration.

Essie Stripling Burnworth, of Potomac, with some success whipped up batches of a "hypo-virulent soup" with which to inject the cankers. Essie Burnworth was a systems analyst and information technology specialist who worked on the lunar landing and chestnut trees, and was instrumental in the University of Maryland Biotechnology Institute's American Chestnut Loaner Lab (d. Feb 2012).

One big stressed family: beech, oak, chestnut, chinkapin.

There were thought to be 4 billion American chestnuts in America in 1900. By the 1940s only a few fully mature clumps of trees remained in their old range. A new stock crossed with the resistant Chinese chestnut has been recently introduced. The original parasite came over with Japanese chestnuts.

~

Mono-layered leafers like the beech avoid blocking out each other's light by forming a jigsaw-like pattern to capture the light. The leaf's orientation is adjustable. Solar energy engineers have been studying this phenomenon.

Being shade-tolerant is no drawback in a forest.

Masting requires much energy.

Masting is much affected by weather.

Seedlings follow mast years.

The beech is listed as among those (relatively) resistant to sulfur dioxide but (painfully) susceptible to frost and salt.

When a mass of shoots grows from a single point, a deformity occurs known as
witch's broom.

~

The coppers are mainly raised from seed,   Bill Hirst, Highland Hill Farm

but they are not reliable seed to seed. If you raise a grafted one, you'll get a uniform color. I'm going to give you to my son Michael. He has a degree in horticulture.   Ibid

I would say without a doubt that Providence, RI, is the copper beech capital of America.   Ibid

~

We respirate. They transpirate.

When it comes to browsing the crepuscular,

white-tailed deer are not inclined. Here and there a nibble.

Does that have to do with the copper color.

No! Deer are color blind!

Not color blind! Deer see only blue.

The beech does not see blue.

For developmental purposes, I understand, the blue end of the spectrum is needed.

The beech disdains wet clay.

~

One claim to the invention of movable type belongs to Laurens Janszoon Coster between 1423 and 1440. Recently, the title has shifted back to Gutenberg.

Coster was alleged to have cut letters for children out of beechwood. When he wrapped the letters in parchment, they left impressions on the parchment, giving him the idea of movable type. Historians now argue there was no such man as Laurens Janszoon Coster, leaving the proud citizens of Haarlem bereft.

No one is disputing that the beech played an inspirational role.

For cathedrals as well.

~

I found this woo-woo list associating the beech with:
the creative
those with good taste and concerned about their looks
the materialistic
those averse to risk
those with good organization of their lives and careers
the reasonable
those who make splendid lifetime companions
the forever young

Remember:
No tree has so fair a bole and so handsome an *instep* as the beech.   Thoreau

And this overstuffed description from *Out of the Woods: The Armchair Guide to Trees,* of the beech looking like a woman who "has just emerged from a wax and a massage"… like a woman who works out, takes care of herself, and maybe even gets a bit of botox (paraphrase by Nancy Ross Hugo).

(Only of late has it been discovered that the earwig has an extra penis in the event some harm should befall the first [*LF*]. And a woman at the local nursery tells me she heard of a certain aphid that was born pregnant. What next.)

~

Peasants were often charged for *pannage,* permitting their pigs to feed on the mast.

They could nab some limbs for fuel, but the trunks belonged to the landholder. It is ventured the taking of limbs reached with a hook or shepherd's crook is the source of the term *by hook or by crook.*

The mere mention of the circumstance above recalls the pigeons' plight in the beech trees from Scottish-born John Muir's *Story of My Boyhood and Youth:*

> *I have seen flocks streaming south in the fall so large that they were flowing over from horizon to horizon in an almost continuous stream all day long, at the rate of forty or fifty miles an hour, like a mighty river in the sky, widening, contracting, descending like falls and cataracts, and rising suddenly here and there in huge ragged masses like high-plashing spray....*

> *"Oh, what bonnie, bonnie birds!" we exclaimed over the first that fell into our hands. "Oh, what colors! Look at their breasts, bonnie as roses, and at their necks aglow wi' every color juist like the wonderfu' wood ducks. Oh, the bonnie, bonnie creatures, they beat a'! Where did they a' come fra, and where are they a'gan? It's awfu' like a sin to kill them!"*

Wrote the great naturalist.

Does that not hurt here, here, and here. Such bonnie, bonnie birds.

Leaving inches of their doo-doo below the branches, if they should live so long as to deliver one last plop.

A project of de-extinction of the passenger pigeon is currently being carried out collaboratively by labs at UC Santa Cruz, Harvard, and Roslin Institute in Scotland. I know scientists attempt these things because they can possibly, probably be done. But how long once done before they end up on our menus all over again.

(We had a memorable meal with friends overlooking the Templo Mayor in Mexico, DF. One dish was of ant eggs. Large eggs, considering the source. We were told the ants buried them in tunnels in which rattlers like to hole up; so extracting them was *muy peligroso.* What appetite I already lacked for this delicacy was scoured out with that tender bit. There is something supremely strange about what our kind bring to table. The sight of Aztec ruins still being excavated in the throbbing heart of a city of so many millions, that was something else again.)

~

Here among the redwoods, these giants get about a third of their water from morning fog, that's a lot of fog to absorb from the surface of their leaves, saving on the amount that must be drawn from the roots up.

Fog has been declared and shown by satellite to be in decline. Fog! The tule ground fog on which the almonds, pistachios, cherries, apricots, and more depend is vanishing.

Drought forced old-growth redwood park-closures in the summer of 2014, the first since the former logging sites were acquired by San Mateo County.

Colin Tudge notes that staying alive is the tree's main business; then comes reproduction. The latter involves sacrifice. Many parents would concur.

~

The leaves may not *absciss* for they are *marcescent.* May wither but not detach in winter.

Also trees grown near streetlights perceive longer days and hold their leaves later.

The *abscission zone* is at the base of the leaf. Once blocked, cutting off nutrients, a tear line forms, the leaf falls.

~

According to the gospel of Bach flower remedies, the beech personality is: judgmental, critical, arrogant, and tense. (Mea culpa. And I know others with the same affliction.) George Bernard Shaw's Professor Higgins has been cited as a prime example of the beech personality. Tolerance, sympathy, and understanding are also told to flow from the remedy.

The tree's essence brings confidence in self-expression (may or may not apply to public speaking).

When Edward Bach developed his remedy, in the 1930s, the formula consisted of a smidgen of flower matter, in a half-and-half mix of brandy and water. It was the dew on the flower he believed to contain the healing property. In lieu of the arduous task of collecting such a quantity of dew, the flowers were steeped in water in the sun.

This is a load of hooey, but anything's worth a shot for a few drops of that loving feeling.

~

The wood of the beech is somewhat plain unless infected by a fungus, and then *spalted,* with dramatic black streaking over the cut planes.

Spalting is mostly found in dead trees. Stressed trees are also susceptible. It can take the form of sap stain, white rot, or zone lines. Furniture makers can turn criminal given these conditions.

Figure in the wood, is good grain gone wild.   Spike Carlsen

When my craftsman son talks about the figure in the wood… it is not exactly a rapture, but not far from one. His hands have changed, he says, his hands are tools in and of themselves.

~

A landmark tree stood at the Scaean Gate of Troy.

This is the beech under which the shepherd Tityrus lay tootling his reed in Virgil's opening Eclogue.

Tityre, tu patulae recubans sub tegmine fagi,
Sylvestrem tenui Musam meditaris avenâ   *Bucolics*

Crescent illae, crescetis amores. As these letters grow, so our love.

Of course someone had to come along and say, wasn't a beech after all.

Then a Victorian with the surname Beeching came to defend its identity:

Thy name of old was great: / What though sour critics teach / "The beech by the Scaean gate / Was not indeed a beech," / That sweet Theocritus / The ilex loved, not thee?— / These are made glorious / Thro' thy name, glorious tree. // And sure 'twas 'neath thy shade / Tityrus oft did use / (The while his oxen strayed) / To meditate the Muse…. On and on he poeticized.

~

Before the city parks, rural cemeteries were part of the picturesque landscape movement.

Mount Auburn Cemetery, 1831, the first "rural cemetery" in America and setting of numerous outstanding beeches.

Before beeches leaf out, bluebells carpet the ground around them in spring.

According to a book someone gifted me in Little Rock, *Fieldbook of American Wildflowers,* annotated with fine-pointed cedar pencil and fountain pen, the dainty bluebell, also commonly called harebell (*Campanula rotundifolia*), can survive at over 5,000 feet. Their first set of round leaves are gone before they flower. The flowers' primary visitor is the bumblebee, which must "clasp the prominent stigma before he can enter the inverted bell" and in getting there dusts off pollen from another flower, initiating cross-fertilization. The observer's note says the flowers were seen among the rocks on the north shore of Lake Superior. (Not where I would expect them found.)

A poet in Cambridge, MA, walks through Mount Auburn Cemetery on her way to work and sent a photo of just such a breathtaking occurrence, bluebells under the canopy, so familiar to the beech woods of England.

The ashes of poet Robert Creeley (1926–2005) are buried under a beech at Mount Auburn Cemetery, Cambridge, MA:

> Look
> at
> the
> light
> of
> this
> hour.

The word trimmed back to the last fore-bearing leaf. Onward, Bob.

(When I dispatched photographer Denny Moers to get a shot of Creeley's tree, his tripod fell over on the poet's stone, breaking the back plate of his camera. After he uncovered the broken part in the mast, he rushed back to his car to see whether he had something—masking tape, Band-Aid or rubber band he could use to secure the plate and finish his shoot in the vanishing light. He found only a pack of old condoms. Wrapped one around the camera, took aim and called it a day. Safe to say, Bob would have liked that. His widow, Penelope, told Denny that Bob & Co. had chugged over the Pyrenees by pissing into the gas tank.)

A Brookline, MA, developer planted what are among the oldest *Fagus sylvatica* in America, a few miles from Mount Auburn, at Longwood Mall. On Google Maps the beech trees flare right up in your face with a speech balloon that says: Really amazing trees. Ancient huge beeches with really climbable branches! (And I am almost blown into them.)

~

Among North American beeches, *Fagus grandifolia,* the most renowned carving:

D. Boon
Cilled
A Bar
On this Tree
In Year 1760.

However, it is long disputed whether the carving was by Daniel Boone, as some scholars doubt he was altogether literate. The tree fell in 1916.

A receipt shows he *could* spell b-e-a-r and joinhand his name ending with *e.*

A person writing in 1884 said that the lettered section had been cut out but disappeared during the Civil War.

It stood on Old Stage Road between Blountville and Jonesborough, TN. Estimated to be 365 years of age.

Another source says the trunk section with Boone's carving is safeguarded in the Filson Historical Society, Louisville. The Historical Society's curator demurs:

Dear Ms. Wright,

That isn't our Boone tree. Ours was supposedly carved in 1803 on a beech tree in what is now Iroquois Park in south Louisville. We do not believe it is authentic. It's most likely a late 19th century fraud—perhaps done by that fine Brown University grad Reuben T. Durrett. Boone was literate and every authentic signature of his I've seen does include the "e" in Boone. If you'd like to see an image of it I can send you one. Good luck with your project. —Jim Holmberg

According to another writer on the topic, carvings from Boone's brother Edward and hunting friend Micajah Callaway appear on another beech. The tree reportedly lives on in a soybean field on Old Medina Road, Madison Co., TN. A someday destination.

∼

The European beeches don't care for city life. They tolerate it. (The Americans less.)

The Europeans are hardier than the Americans, grow faster, and withstand crummier dirt.

American beeches resist transplanting. Europeans are more obliging.

∼

Known as a wolf tree, one whose dominance inhibits the growth of small trees around it.

Morels grow in beech woods. Truffles on their roots. Two pluses.

The excrement of beech aphids is referred to as *honeydew black*. Mmm-hmm.

The bug is a mule for the fungus (*LF*).

~

The beech does not produce secondary buds. Speculation is that this may be the reason it hangs on to its leaves through winter, protecting that single set of buds.

One Vermont forester offers reasons why it holds its leaves until spring: to provide mulch in the spring, to discourage deer,
to trap snow for more moisture in spring, or it is just not fully evolved as a deciduous tree.

The beech hedge for instance might remain a juvenile due to early and regular
       pruning.

All theory, dear friend, is grey, but the golden tree of actual life springs ever green—
sayeth Mephistopheles to the student. Goethe, an above-average plant man.

~

Beech bonsai.
They exist!
declared Rowan.
The *F. crenata*
and *F. japonica*
lend themselves
to this specialty.

~

Resilient fighters, the beech, says Olavi Huikari, who also tells us a full half of our DNA is held in common with them. *Half.*

A photograph of a tree with a ghoulish mien was taken by a man dropping his mother off to work. It reminded him of Edvard Munch's *The Scream.* The reporter likened it to the Whomping Willow in Harry Potter or an enchanted Disney forest. Referred to as an "unsightly work of nature." Is not the tree being treated as *lifelike* and the media being treated as *living.*

~

On Miners Castle Road (MI) over 200 sick beeches were cut down in June 2014. Reportedly to protect visitors in the event of a blowdown. The city has been instructed that the felled ones remain on the ground that they return to the biomass.

The map of beech-bark-diseased trees appears pretty catastrophic for New England's beeches. (Brings to mind the New Orleans Parish online murder map. Likewise the map of California wildfires.)

Resistance to beech bark disease has been attributed to bark anatomy. About 1 percent are resistant. *1%.*

~

A spontaneous protest often arises when some agency in some locale determines a beech, especially its bulging, aboveground roots, to be a hazard. A venerable Belfast beech was recently granted a temporary stay of execution. The engineers arrived with a crane but backed down after a neighborhood confrontation, with the warning that the crane would return.

Was once common to compose a poem to stay the saw: Spare, woodman, spare the beechen tree ("The Beech Tree's Petition," 1805). This the single most notable instance, by Thomas Campbell. On and on he intoned.

~

Under the beeches, beechdrops get their sugars directly from the tree roots.

Beechdrops, a broomrape (*Epifagus virginiana*), grows at the base of American and European beeches. An obligate parasite, feeding only on beech sap from the roots. Doesn't photosynthesize. Has a flower at the top that must be pollinated by insects and a closed flower lower down on the stem that is self-fertilizing. In other words, it's covered. As an annual, beechdrops do nominal harm to their hosts.

Used for bowel infections. Or not.

Can be applied to gangrene.

Flying squirrels (*Glaucomys volans*) are nocturnal, love beechnuts, and are fond of nesting in their old hollows and dining on the fungi of their dying wood.

~

Glee Gum of Providence, RI, uses a natural sweetener from the beech, xylitol (also in berries, plums, mushrooms, lettuce, birch, and corncobs). Unlike sugar-sweetened gums, xylitol creates an alkaline environment that resists tooth decay and promotes remineralization of tooth enamel. Some studies indicate that it decreases incidence of middle-ear infections and infections originating in the mouth. Discovered by German chemist Emil Fischer in 1890 and French chemist M.G. Bertrand (the German got the credit). During the sugar shortage of WWII it started being used widely.

Xylitol is highly poisonous to dogs. Don't give them Glee Gum. Only to stoners would it occur to give a dog chewing gum.

Though my adult self dislikes gum (Frances Mayes told me, It's vulgar), I bought a pack of Glee Gum. Not too sweet, hardens quickly. My humanoid kid-self liked Double Bubble, Juicy Fruit, Dentyne, Blackjack, and Beech-Nut gum, the flavors of which linger vividly. Mamo always gave me half a stick of Juicy Fruit to settle me down in church, with my head in her lap as she stroked my hair and the preacher went berserk. Bapo sang in the choir with his hearing aid off; so he missed the brimstone business while his mind spun out into baseball statistic–land.

~

The Tsalagi (Cherokee) raided the chipmunks' stashes of beechnuts so they didn't have to gather, cull, or hull them, it is written in *The Meaning of Trees*. Where I come from, that's cheating.

~

Between 600 and 800 people were killed by the hurricane of 1938, 317 of them Rhode Islanders. 275 million trees went down that night. It was a full equinox moon. Highest tide of the year. Rhode Island was slammed by the right-front quadrant. Full force. A light rain had been forecast for that early fall evening.

~

Could be a sunscreen, having low photosynthetic capacity.

Could be a repellent, avoided by leaf-cutter ants and other herbivores.

~

Anthocyanin is the pigment that causes beeches to be purple and strawberries red. Greek *anthos* (flower), *kyanos* (dark blue).

At the former convent of the Presentation Sisters on Ireland's Dingle Peninsula, the hues of the copper that shelters the nuns' graves are felt to evoke the blood of Christ.

~

The Oxford room of Gerard Manley Hopkins overlooked a beech, cut to create more light for a few of his dormitory fellows. This dogged the poet/priest for the rest of his days.

When not climbing the elm in his parents' yard, boy Gerard's idea of glory was a beech at his grandparents' house in Croydon.

~

Joyce Kilmer was paid $6 for "Trees" when it appeared in *Poetry,* August 1913. It is at long last fading from the curriculum. Though the rest stop on the New Jersey Turnpike in his name hums right along. (Kilmer was taken out by a sniper in the Second Battle of the Marne, 1918, age 31.)

~

In accordance with 11th-century English law, a beech became a *deodand* (gift to god) when it fell on a woman and splattered her brains. By law the owner had to give the tree to the state or pay its value, 16 pence, to the town. Brains, assigned no ordinal value.

An Arkansas man was killed by a falling beech in the Ozark–St. Francis National Forest in 1993 working for a contractor hired by the forest service to cull trees. His wife sued the feds for choosing a bad contractor.

~

Coppers are *sports* or *quirks:* not a real true species.

Buchstaben, the German word for letters, "beech stick."

The leaves fatten dormice (once a delicacy).

Thrushes. Turkey. Grouse.

Pliny claimed the nuts make hogs brisk and lively and render the flesh tender for
cooking.

Palmerius claimed the ancient *fāgos* was not a beech but an oak.

The nuts eaten raw will almost guarantee a stomachache. For that kind of trouble it
would be more gratifying to devour the magic mushroom.

Half the nut is oil, quarter of that protein; half fat. Good serving of carbs.

If your animals are chewing the fence posts, they could use some beech-
leaf fodder.

~

Early settlers didn't go about planting ornamental trees.

American beeches came down lickety-split under the blades of 18th- and 19th-century farmers. The trees indicated rich, loamy soil.

Plus, there was the terror factor of what was out there in the impenetrable gloom.

Better to see the space beyond the space than lack thereof.

The oil kept better than oil of the olive.

~

Beech mast was once *buck;* thus Buckingham County. In Buckinghamshire, England, beechwood furniture is made.

Hard to split when green; splits too readily when dry.

Decays quickly in the atmosphere. (Or as I was told bluntly, If you don't want wrinkles, live in space.)

Flourishes in chalky, sandy soil.

89th on the list of important forest trees of the US, *Fagus grandifolia.*

From the foliage, much potash.

When the wood is so dry it crumbles, it's punk.

Good for tinder.

Fell in summer when the sap is in full circulation.

Limbs low.

~

It has been remarked that the spreading beech and the tall beech are the Adonis and Hercules of our Sylvas. The attribution has been so various I have no idea who was on first. Annie Oakes Huntington (who wrote on trees in winter as well as poison ivy and sumac) attributed it to Mathews, no doubt such an illustrious figure in his time that the rest of his name was assumed.

It makes a stately tree, wrote Batty Langley of Twickenham in 1728. *Stately,* as the celebrated novel begins. *Stately,* as the less-attended day-long poem *Midwinter Day,* by Bernadette Mayer, begins. Stately, the beeches are.

~

The Burnham Beeches enjoyed "undivided sovereignty" over other species for many a generation. At one time so impenetrable, they were notorious for harboring bandits, until the 12th Abbot of St. Albans began cutting them back.

Francis George Heath was instrumental in sparing Burnham Beeches from development; in failing to persuade the Crown to buy the woods and set it aside for the public, convinced the city of London to do so, including an allowance for its maintenance. Victoria Park Act of 1872 preserved the woods by law. Actual thinking forward.

Francis George Heath quoting the 18th-century landscape "theorist" and watercolorist (Father) William Gilpin: the hanging spray [in winter] of the Beech, in old trees especially, is often twisted and intermingled disagreeably, and has a perplexed, matted appearance. The whole tree gives us something of the idea of an entangled head of bushy hair....

Gilpin is among those identified as an originator of "the picturesque" or "that kind of beauty which is agreeable in a picture."

Burnham Beeches, reported to have been pollarded by Cromwell's soldiers.
      (Unconfirmed.)

No *estovers,* rights to take the wood from land not owned. Top-lopping in Burnham
      Beeches, lord of the manor's privilege alone.

Of Birnam Wood let Scotland talk
      While we've our Burnham Beeches.   Henry Luttrell

(An oak, upheld with crutches, is made out to be the last of the trees that Malcolm III's soldiers used as disguise against Macbeth.)

The movie industry closes in on Burnham Beeches for location shoots: Robin Hood, Harry Potter, Snow White, James Bond. You name it. Restricted to 20 days a year of filming.

Scribblers and other idlers have long found their way under Burnham's deep shade, or more probably, found themselves imagining themselves thus propped:

There at the foot of yonder nodding beech,
     That wreathes its old fantastic roots so high,
His listless length at noontide would he stretch,
     And pore upon the brook that babbles by.   Thomas Gray

Gray's "Elegy Written in a Country Churchyard" was composed on the fringe of these woods at the wonderfully named Stoke Poges churchyard, though one enters by way of a lane "umbrageous with elms." The History Hut edges up to the woods where George Grote sketched out his 12-vol *History of Greece.*

~

A couple in Warwick Neck, RI, have several beeches of which they are justifiably proud. One in particular, the larger, the copper with its fused trunk. Their fern-leaf also has a fused trunk, one that opens up and then re-fuses.

When the elder son was a teen he bought an old Jeep, then a second to harvest its parts. He raised the body from the chassis suspended from the fern-leaved. His father said, "You've got one day," though it took several and several more. They adamantly spared the copper the load. A forester friend from New Hampshire was going to bore the copper for age, but decided better of it and rough-guessed 200 years. While a fungus had developed in an opening, the forester said, Leave her be. If the couple has an event, they rope the copper off so cars cannot approach. A middle-aged man stopped by after a wedding, told the current owners he grew up there, but seeing that they were having a celebration, he would come another time. They sensed his eye linger on the beech and perhaps attendant memories.

Because the roots are aboveground the neighborhood dogs drink from pools formed in the cavities of those great haunches, as if at a trough.

That too, tree people have come to think is a good thing, to let the water stand.

My friend Ellie in Cranston, RI, just beyond the Providence line, has a beech. The only growing thing in her backyard. The kids had a tree house. They used to sleep in it though daughter Sophie was a sleepwalker. They were awakened late into a night by a crashing and moaning, and husband Bill rushed out to rescue his daughter entangled in a rope ladder amid the copper's trusty branches.

~

If the tree runs out of carbs, it starves.

If the ropes of water molecules are broken by heat and the tension that causes,

the tree dies of thirst.

The *New York Times* reported that a recent study found that 70 percent of 226 forest species from 81 sites worldwide now live on the edge of… hydraulic failure. *70%.*

~

The coppers "are commonly planted and admired by many, reviled by some."

Reviled?

According to one Alan Mitchell, their heavy dark masses are garish without being bright, blending with nothing, contrasting pleasantly with nothing, absorbing light uselessly; most are a blot on the landscape all summer long. Seconded by a Hugh Johnson: They have their (very brief) springtime moment of freshness, but I agree that most are a blot on the landscape all summer long.

I give you Donald Culross Peattie, who abandoned French poetry for the forest, at the beginning of his beech tree chapter: A beech is, in almost any landscape where it appears, the finest tree to be seen.

He possessed what Verlyn Klinkenborg describes as "an arboretum of the mind."

~

Before the last glaciation, their domain included all of the continental US. Now they are Eastern trees though they show up on range maps in Utah.

~

I read that city workers were cutting down poisoned oak trees at Toomer's Corner, entrance to Auburn University, Auburn, AL. The perp is serving a jail term (length unspecified) for pleading guilty to poisoning the trees.

A replica of one of Toomer's Oaks has been built in California, shipped to and reassembled in Auburn, where it stands inside Auburn Art.

They were poisoned at the end of a bad football season. Rationale offered, "He just had too much 'Bama in him."

According to the manufacturer of Spike® 80DF, 100 parts per billion would be lethal to a live oak; the highest sample was 51 parts per million. "Do no harm in remediation," was the University's mantra. Two years of treatment followed. The trees were damned. In keeping with the school's tradition, the trees were rolled with toilet paper before coming down. 83,000 attended last rites in a town of 57,000. "Everyone wanted a piece: of branch, of bark, of leaf." Beech, oak, chestnut, chinkapin. A fecund and vulnerable extended family.

Recollect giving a midday reading at Auburn. The school had the unusual status of being a state liberal arts college. When I visited, it had recently been featured in a *NYT Magazine* article on philosophy professor Kelly Jolley, "The Thinker," who with his colleagues had made philosophy the most popular major on campus. It would be worth sticking around to see what the philosophers of Auburn are thinking decades hence (perhaps the only college in the land where philosophy is the #1 concentration. Too much 'Bama?).

~

An outstanding fern leaf on State Street in Warren, RI, holds dominion over its own lot. A bench just outside its drip line invites passersby to enjoy it. The residents of the rambling colonial who own the beech bought the house, they mused, because of the tree; now they have to maintain the house.

~

The first Rhode Island governor is buried in Juniper Hill, in Bristol, RI, a cemetery abundant in beeches. His daughter married a future senator and that senator was great-great-grandfather of Charles Gibson, of the Gibson girls, an idealization of how girls were supposed to look, the first American pinups. The Gibson house in Bristol is a wreck. Totaled. As long as we have lived here renovations have been threatened but never undertaken or once undertaken, quickly abandoned. Trees came down. Struts came down. How the house stands is hard to fathom.

John Campanini of the Rhode Island Tree Council declares he knows under exactly which tree he would be seated and what he would be drinking if he knew he was about to die. I know it was a fern leaf and a bench was already present, but I am not sure that the one on State Street in Warren is the one he held in his mind's eye. It might just be in mine. Sweater weather. I would bring a book, but would not even pretend to read.

~

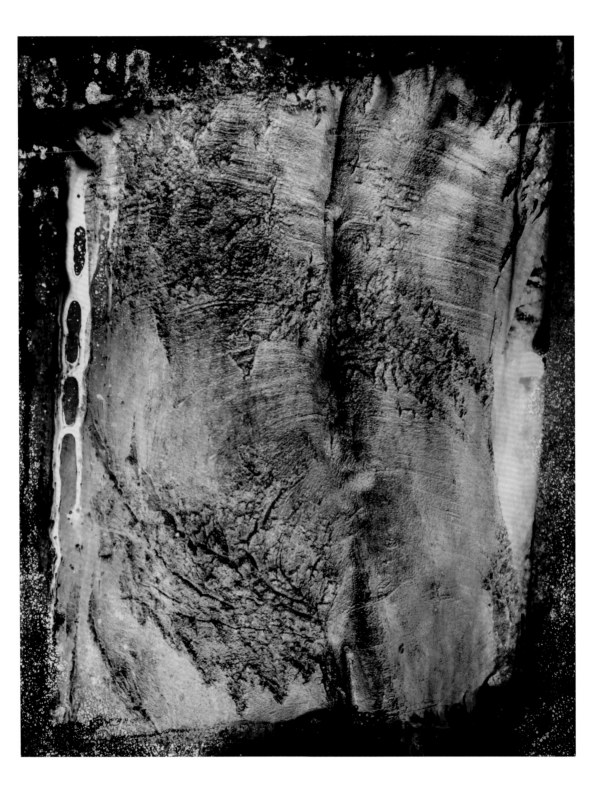

Two expeditions to Japan, in 1853 and 1854, broke *Sakoku,* the isolation policy in place since the middle of the 17th century. Whether they returned with *Fagus sieboldii,* that is *F. crenata,* or *Fagus japonica* (blue beech or dog buna or black buna), I am uncertain. It must be local lore that European beech seeds were collected on Commodore Perry's black ships, at least with respect to them coming from the Pacific East. The first *F. sieboldii* (from Japan) seeds were brought by the Arnold Arboretum's director, Charles Sprague Sargent, in 1893. *F. japonica* seeds came shortly thereafter.

∼

It is not valued as a highly utilitarian tree. However, its practical applications, past and present, constitute a big list:

A–C

acetate

axle-trees of chariots (not in high demand)

barrels

bentwood furniture

blister treatment

boat planking

book binding (in lieu of pasteboard)

bowls, spoons, plates

butter from the nut in Silesia (raise your hand if you know where Silesia is)

carpenter planes

carriage panels (likewise fallen into disuse)

charcoal

coffee (the nuts when roasted, an agreeable substitute for coffee)

containers

corn shovels

crates

creosote

crossties

culverts (once upon a time, the old and hollow ones served)

D–H

dens (for squirrels, raccoons, opossums)

divining rods

drums (with a tone between maple and birch)

dyes

eco-fabric (Modal® from sustainable harvested forests, Austria)

expectorant

eye cream (extract from the bud, for its flavonoids, peptides, etc.)

eyewash (Ojibwa)

fellies (in wheels, you know, fellies)

fining agent for Budweiser (from the chips)

flooring

flour (Potawatomi, Iroquois, Menominee, Ojibwa—the last reported to
have stolen the caches of deer mice)

food (for creatures large and small: birds, white-tailed deer, flying
squirrels, foxes, grouse, pheasant, bear, porcupines, swine

food storage (doesn't transfer the smell)

fuel

fuel

fuel (and then along came coal)

galley (blessedly in disuse)

gondola oars (Even Providence, RI, boasts three restored Venetian gondolas
for the WaterFire on the river, otherwise, outside of Venice and Las Vegas,
seldom seen. The oar makers, the *remèri,* a vanishing vocation.)

granary shovels

gudgeons (and bearings in grist and saw mills)

gun butts

handles (for tools and brushes)

J–O

joinery

keels (of wooden ships, the heaviest piece of wood on the ship; whereas
oak is bound to split if it hits rock, the beech leaks. Affirmed by
remains of a 5th-century ship.)

lager (from a domestic yeast in Bavaria since the 15th century; fused to an
imported yeast thought to be from a tidbit of beechwood in the gut
of a fruit fly. The combined yeasts enable cold fermentation.
Scientists have narrowed the journeying morsel to a wild yeast
from the beech forests of Patagonia.)

liqueur (beechleaf noyau)

luxury linens (Italian)

mallet heads

mattress stuffing

(*lits de parlement,* talking beds, to the French peasants: *But there is yet another benefit which this Tree presents us ; that its very leaves… afford the best and easiest* Mattresses *in the world to lay under our* Quilts *instead of* Straw *; because, besides their tenderness and loose lying together, they continue sweet for seven or eight years long, before which time* Straw *becomes* musty *and hard ; they are thus used by divers persons of quality in* Dauphine *; and in* Switzerland *I have sometimes lain on them to my great refreshment ; so as of this Tree it may properly be said, The wood's an House ; the leaves a Bed.* John Evelyn)

methanol production

mortars and pestles

nests for chickadees

oil (for lamps)

oil (from the nut, which François André Michaux insisted is next in fineness
to that of the olive)

P–Y

paper filler

piano paneling

pigment (from its soot, bistre)

plywood

poison ivy wash (from north side of the bark)

poultice for burns, from leaves of beech and linden in equal portion (Iroquois)

pulp (for making cardboard)

railroad ties

sabot shoes (French clog, for the peasant class)

salad green (from fresh leaf)

saddle tree

sandals

scabbard cores (the poplar now preferred if your sword has worn out
its old one)

sink (for soil nitrogen)

skin toner (from the French Riviera)

smoking herrings

snuff boxes

sweetener

tanning leather (in a decoction from the bark)

tea for lungs

tobacco substitute (The Germans tried to fob beech leaf off on WWI
soldiers in lieu of the real thing. That didn't go over any more than
smoking grapevine.)

toothpicks (provided by the spiky buds)

toys (I would not bet on the success of a pull toy of beech for a
toddler's handheld electronic game)

treatment (for swellings, including varicose veins)

turnery

veneer

wagon wheels (still made at Louisiana State Prison, Angola, primarily for
their funeral caissons)

water wheels (*This noble Timber is of such a Nature, that if it's kept
always wet, or always dry, 'twill last for many Ages; but if it
happens to be often wet and dry, 'tis presently rotten and useless.*
Batty Langley, of Twickenham, 1728)

Windsor chairs (the turned parts)

wrest plank in pianos (to which the tuning pin is attached)

wrinkle remover

Yule logs (which along with mistletoe comes to us from the pagans)

"Culminating—for humility—in the lowly clothespin," adds the dapper and dedicated Donald Culross Peattie, who also tagged it a second-rate utilitarian tree.

Chewing the leaves is recommended to help you rid yourself of worms.

Not a cure for cancer, but does not mean the claim hasn't been made. (The bark of the Pacific yew however…)

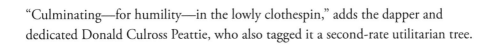

What was not anticipated was the Miura fold. In 2009 Japanese scientist Koryo Miura conceived of a way to fold an array of solar panels into a space satellite by mimicking beech leaves unfolding from the bud (when it is time for them to begin absorbing energy), a complication on the accordion fold. Further applications include a subway map and heart stents.

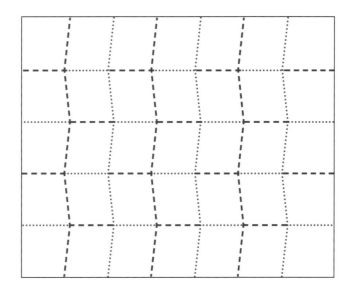

~

The Manataka American Indian Council site says beech bark tea cures vomiting (with the caveat, inadvisable to brew before consulting your own physician). The American Indian Heritage Support Center lists the Manataka as a fraudulent association. Don't pay for a sweat lodge session or vision quest with this outfit.

~

It is a big part of my day to see that tree [a copper], says the owner of a coffee shop in Troutdale, OR.

Planted by a farmer in 1885, the tree is threatened by the building of a park. When Mt. Hood Community College bought up part of Alfred Baker's land, the tree was spared and named in his honor. The city owns the land and has ordered a fence be built to protect it during construction.

~

Along the northern front infected trees can go from a vigour rating of 1 (healthy) to 5 (dead) in one year!   John McLaughlin

The twice-stabbed lady beetle feeds on the scale. (*LF.*) In Ontario where it is indigenous.

Lepidoptera caterpillars that eat beech leaves include the ghost moth, the American white admiral, emperor moth, walnut sphinx, pale November moth, feathered thorn, common wave, and many many more.

The Europeans are faulted for the American beeches' falling to bark scale disease. It is thought they brought it with them when imported for landscaping. Bark scale was first found in Canada's Maritime provinces in the 1920s. The insect is Lilliputian but can pierce the bark, an invitation for the fungus (*N. coccinea* aka *LF*). Other invaders follow. Beech snap can be the result, the great trees breaking off abruptly a short distance up the trunk.

~

The Americans can handle the cold a bit better; the Europeans can take the heat.

Tannin makes your mouth dry and pucker.

The Europeans are well represented in the arboretum of Echo, Oregon.

Portland boasts nine *Fagus sylvatica* and one weeper.

The largest copper in Seattle is on a side of the Asian Art Museum. Its plaque was stolen. Arthur Lee Jacobson's Seattle tree walks continue rain or shine, and the one opportunity I had to join one, the downpour held me to my hotel room slowly turning pages.

So much for Texas as the current western range.

~

There is a variety in northeastern Mexico about which I know nothing, other than the tree no longer holds the status of its own species (as Christopher is no longer a saint) but has been renamed a variant of *F. grandifolia.* (And Christopher was just a good guy as guys go.)

~

In Germany, remnant beech forests are to be declared part of the world's natural heritage.

In the Carpathians, 30,000 have been granted this status by UNESCO.

In Tacitus's time, the copper beech was the dominant tree of Germania.

In Westphalia, babies were said to come from the hollow of the beech. No stork involved.

There the beech is used to smoke their hams. No connection between babies and smoked hams.

~

Beech hedges last for centuries. Centuries. Tall ladies on tall ladders must be
employed to trim them.

The most renowned is the Meikleour Hedge in Scotland planted in 1745. Stands
up to 120 feet. Richard Mabey tells us that those planting it left abruptly to fight,
leaving their tools under the hedge. The Jacobite who initiated the planting was
killed in battle a year later and his widow was driven out, but the descendants are
back.

From what I've heard, you can prune whenever you want, once the hedge is
established.

Mabey tells of another, on the estate of Cameron of Lochiel, whereby the trees
were laid in at an angle, before planting, when the men were called to fight in 1715.
The men never returned to correct their position so the hedge grew up slantingly.

In Belgium, trellised beech hedges are known to be quite elegant, planted a few inches apart and bound in their early development by osiers until they graft together. So osiers and beeches *are* related. This is an old, specific, country skill.

In County Antrim, Northern Ireland, there is a landmark tunnel of beeches, the Dark Hedges, planted in the mid-18th century by the Stuart family. Other references list them as 300 years old. Pictures of them would make a romantic out of a rock.

Close to Stonehenge, the Nile Clumps beech trees were planted by the 6th Marquess of Queensberry to commemorate the British Fleet's victory over Napoleon under Horatio Nelson. The trees are planted in positions to mark those of the British and French ships in the battle. From toy soldiers, to dead soldiers, to reenactor navies of trees.

Escot Gardens Maze (Devon, UK) was designed by Adrian Fisher in 2004 with over 4,000 beech trees. Noah's Ark Zoo Farm (UK) holds the record for the longest maze in Europe, using green beeches for hedges and coppers for the animals.

Here under the banner of Old Glory, we mainly go in for maize mazes.

~

A first-rate avenue tree if you have an avenue or live on one or wish to. Avenue here could mean: a lane to your magnificent house, or where I sit in Petaluma, on a short dead-end street at the terminus of which a man has planted a jumbo sign, END, putting an unambiguous point on not being open-armed to people turning into his driveway.

There is an avenue of beeches on the Forum Road in Dorset, planted in 1835; 365 trees, one for each day.

~

Beech wood was described in 1920 by the British-born keeper of the Arnold Arboretum as being "clad in snug gray satin" and "a modern tree as trees go."

The watersmoothsilversatin bark is an adaptation from its tropical beginnings, fending off the epiphytic plants, and preventing the bark from cracking when the cold days hit by reflecting the sunlight.

E.H. Wilson noted that because the smooth limbs cross and grow into each other, they are speculated to have given rise to the idea of grafting.

~

The male catkins appear in April and are green, pendant, and borne on long stalks. The female flowers are scratchy, oval balls borne on a stem with protruding long slender styles, appearing by May. The female flowers mature 2–3 days before the male flowers. Flowers produce nuts every other or third year. Two nuts to a cupule.

Fagus sylvatica.
Die Mastbuche.

The littlest flowers are unisexual.

It is a Stone Age tree.

An Iron Age tree.

It is an Ice Age tree. According to the pollen record.

Preglacial fossil remains have been found.

There are ages in between.

The evidence is in the peat.

Not introduced by Romans as formerly thought.

To Caesar's claims, pay no mind. (Hence the phrase: full of baloney.)

Indifferent to pH.

There is an allée of them at a convent in Rhode Island.

Inosculated: intertwined and joined together.

Esculent: edible. (Why not just say so.)

DBH = Diameter at Breast Height.

The leaf is oval to obovate.

~

A story persists that in Buch (beech), Switzerland, there were five brothers who slew each other, and five purple beeches sprang up in their stead.

1680 is the oft-cited date of when the copper came about in Buch.

The purple was also reported in the wild in the Vosges.

The shield of the village features a purple beech.

One in 10,000 seedlings may have purple leaves.

(In 1955, Krussmann established that the offspring of the coppers do not run true to type. Heinze and Gerburek were attempting to narrow the trait to a single dominant gene on into 1995.)

It remains the most populous of forest trees in Denmark and the most southern county of Sweden, Skåne.

~

Dispersed by wind. Says one.

Not dispersed by wind. Says another.

Dispersed by wildlife. Says one.

Dispersed by blue jays. Says another.

Not dispersed by jays. Says one.

~

The blue jay, the only bird that caches nuts in the ground.

Not entirely true, they are simply the best at it. Nor are all jays blue. Nor in truth are any blue.

Blue jay reflecting and scattering its blue, winging and caching its nuts, foresting us with oaks and beeches (and in the case of the Steller's jays, pines). Bless their raucous, cheery souls. Jay, from the Latin *gallus,* gay.

Only 1 percent are egg robbers. *1%.*

One was observed burying 2,000 beechnuts in one month.

~

The picturesque landscape movement in 19th-century America ushered in the planting of *Fagus sylvatica,*

but a Swedish botanist claimed to have seen them near Philadelphia in 1748.

~

Fastigiata: columnar.

Osculate: one limb shares a common tangent with another curve at point of contact. It's geometry.

Frass: entomology, larvae doo-doo. Creates a tinkling as it falls through the foliage in impressive quantity. In the case of the beech, it might be from an ambrosia beetle, esp the *Platypus* (ambrosia) and the Columbian timber beetle (*Corthylus columbianus*). There are other boring contenders.

Artfully they ramify.

The beech is a coolant.

Branches that have been grafted to each other are pleached.

Some call the treetop infundibular, but I don't see it.

Limbs low.

Early fall: husks open.

~

I have waited in traffic in Holland while pigs snuffled beech mast off the road.   Colin Tudge

~

In London:
Staying in a hotel across the street from Kensington Gardens. They are building an arena for the coming Rolling Stones concert. An amble to the weeping beech under which Peter Pan slept after he escaped the nursery. Bedtime stories too have living physical landmarks. The tree renders Peter sort of credible.

The Upside Down Tree is chained off. Children can't resist disappearing under the cascade. Even if I do not make it to Kew Gardens on this trip, it is hard to resist looking for the tree that triggers a reset of your entire cosmology.

~

Landmark designation was granted in 1966 to a weeping beech from Belgium planted, 1847, in Flushing, Queens, with a 100-foot iron gate protecting its perimeter. It died in the 1990s. Protection was sought for a copper in Woodside, Queens, in 2012. Outcome unknown.

~

An old forester superstition is that the young ones won't grow unless the parents are removed. Wonder where that notion took root.

Maintenance best when trees are young. The older the tree, the more its growth habits have been set. Similarly familiar.

The beech has to do with thresholds.

Used to mark boundaries.

So Robin Hood and his boys bounded through the beechen woods.

From the murder site of five German brothers, grew five purple beeches.

~

Allow the tree a breather.

They build the world

organically speaking.

A mature beech breathes.

~

Newport again:
Beechwood, the cottage of the Astors, who made their original money in rodent
fur (note the tile beavers in the subway stop at Astor Place in Manhattan). Mrs.
Astor was a real piece of work, but wisely persuaded her husband to drop his
middle name, Backhouse. She liked society. He liked power. He liked yachts with
girls aboard. He liked whiskey and breeding horses. She liked jewels and of an
evening came out encrusted. She liked footmen dressed in blue livery. Both dissed
new wealth, Jews, Irish, Catholics. In time their mansion on 5th Avenue became
a synagogue. For a while the Newport mansion was open to the public. Now it's
back in private hands: Larry Ellison, the CEO of Oracle, plans a museum for his
art collection.

No doubt beech trees are part of the landscape of Beechwood, and at The Breakers,
a 70-room Italian Renaissance-style palazzo, summer cottage of the Vanderbilts
(upon whom the Astors looked firmly down), you will find outstanding specimens.

The Elms is home to many a splendrous weeper,

including one I cannot squeeze entirely inside one frame of my phone.

～

This may belong to the world of xenopsychology, the kind of emotional response attributed to plants referred to as *hormonal sentience*. How sensitive the beech is in this iffy science I doubt has been studied. One undeniable feature: whatever lives, struggles.

～

Beech in the house interferes with a spirit's passing.

Purple Fountain ('Purpurea pendula') has a single straight leader.

'Asplenifolia', that's a fair, fair, fair tree.

There are copper fern leafs but they are a rare rare tree.

Beech in the house prolongs labor.

Most Rohaniis are copper ('Purpurea Rohanii').

The oldest *F. sylvatica* in the Arnold was grown from seed planted in 1875.

Tricolor ('Roseomarginata'): their leaves scorch, and the only one I have seen in Rhode Island was at a nursery, burned by the sun. Advice offered by one nurseryman is "not to baby it." Advocating, in fact, stress, to bring out its colors.

The beech is gregarious, says one.

The beech prefereth its own company, says another.

Never forget: the Beech is all that we want a tree to be.   Donald Culross Peattie

~

Learning that the turned parts of Windsor chairs came from the beeches of the Chilterns, recollect reading about an American who had a semiknowledgeable interest in furniture, and as an acquaintance of an English aristocrat, made the faux pas of commenting (favorably) on the aristocrat's Windsors and was promptly asked to leave. "Damn fellow complimented my chairs"—the presumption. Must have been Hepplewhites. It couldn't have been the democratic Windsor.

Bodgers were those that turned the woods on the spot. Almost onomatopoeic as in the Irish humpers who built roads in the Arkansas Delta. How the Irish came to be in that unforgiving place pulling that thankless detail, I have no idea.

~

Voles can do a lot of damage if they're about. I have never seen one moving around down there, but our neighbor in California has concocted an elaborate assemblage of obstacles to prevent them digging under the fence line. Whether that keeps them on our side or just discourages them from plowing around altogether is unknown.

Richard Mabey describes a drought in the mid-70s in a beechy reserve in the Wye Valley, accompanied by a de-barking campaign on the part of the gray squirrel. Followed the bank voles that killed most of the saplings. The voles were reported to have been so numerous "the ground appeared to be trembling." Our voles are pretty rampant, too, but the marsh dogs, the orange-toothed nutrias, are the ones that cause the banks of the Mississippi to shudder.

Voles have been linked to nephropathia epidemica in Europe. It's all about global warming, baby. When the summers heat up and the winters don't freeze up, there is more mast. With more mast, more voles. In humans this causes fever, headache, back pain, stomach pain, and bleeding. It doesn't usually take you out, but makes you beg to go. Vole droppings, they are in the air. So far: Belgium, Luxembourg, the Netherlands, Sweden, France, Germany are reporting cases.

~

Infamous Los Alamos, town without pity, is now running an intensive-care lab to study how trees die. In a place that has suffered cataclysmic droughts, now that temperatures are rising due to human activity, no rebound is expected, the *NYT* regretfully reported, Christmas before last.

In 2011 a perimeter fire had to be set around the nuclear lab and the RADIOACTIVE MATERIAL STORED THEREIN, to head off the Las Conchas fire. Over 150,000 acres burned. The largest in New Mexico's history (until the following year). Flooding followed as feared. One acre of lab land burned.

Almost every adult has a doctorate and Los Alamos enjoys proximity to Santa Fe's restaurants and shopping. Skiing is down due to limited snowfall. Newcomers are advised to buy land with few trees since they are a fire hazard.

Averring against the "natural" law of forest succession, Richard Mabey writes: In the real world disturbance and compromise, not order, are the rule.

"Naturalness," holds Mabey, "is whatever occurs between human interventions." Naturalness does appear to usher in a backlash.

He also states that age and internal rottenness don't take down a tree. They don't always take down the human form either.

~

In Newport:

I was relieved when I saw that the beech being taken down on Salve Regina's campus was not the magnificent one in the center of the circular drive of McAuley Hall. Despite the ugly cavity in its side at breast height, it's budding out.

McAuley once belonged to a tobacco and real estate heiress. Now named for the founder of the Sisters of Mercy. Both Catherines, heiress and nun.

The tree that came down was by the entrance, near the dolium excavated from an Italian garden. The plain earthenware vase, believed to date from 200 BCE. Newport is laden with beautiful, dense objects. And held aloft by beech trees.

Two grown fern-leaved beeches were brought to Vinland for its owner, Mrs. Catharine Lorillard Wolfe, from a property she also owned on the sound, off New York. It was some kind of operation, entailing: a chartered coal barge, a rented wharf, 8 pairs of horses for each tree, telegraph lines lowered, another boat, a tug, a wintering over in New Haven... They made it. See what I mean, these things are hardy, and tree kin, likewise made of serious sap.

Because of their shallow roots, beeches were often moved, but not such distances.

Chris Fletcher said he surveyed and tagged all 900 of Salve's campus trees with GPS coordinates last year. The college sits in the midst of all that tarnished glory as it is born of 7 former Gilded estates.

~

Fossils have been found in the Antarctic.

The oldest beech *Fagacae* fossil in the US was found in eastern Tennesse.

Robert Gray refers to *the tree* as an electrochemical treatment plant.

Some studies are showing that trees are drawing up less water to adjust to the climate changes going on, as in: less rain, less water in the fields.

Beech scale disease from *C. fagisuga* (*LF*) has claimed many a life.

~

Now the orange trees are in extremis. None are immune to bacterium *C. liberibacter*—brought by a flying insect, an Asian psyllid, that sucks it out of one tree and injects it into another. Pretty nasty (*LF*). Then there is the bacterial citrus greening disease, delightfully named *huanglongbing*, but describing a contagious and terminal cancer. The current plan is to insert a spinach gene coded for a protein that kills the HLB bacteria. To genetically modify or not to modify, that is a worm of a whole 'nother color.

Frankenfood or not, I'll take the transgenic odds over the pesticidal craze any day, any place.

~

They grow among sugar maple, birch, hemlock, white pine, buckeye, white ash, tulip tree, white oak, witch hazel. Sugar maple and beech are common companions.

My experience with sugar maples is limited to Coggeshall Farm in Bristol, RI, a museum of a working farm. It was my first experience of a farm as a museum, which has an executive director, a board, and so forth. They are not uncommon, but a farm was a farm in Arkansas, and in my part of Arkansas, usually a farm meant a poor farm; rocks, the principal crop.

A visit to Ezra Pound's daughter, Mary de Rachewiltz, a few years back, Brunnenburg Castle. The lower level of the castle is an agricultural museum, set up by her son, Siegfried Walter de Rachewiltz, director of the South Tyrolean Museum of History. Mary de Rachewiltz is a magnificent, hyper-articulate, self-possessed, perfect-postured woman—and devoted daughter. I will always be grateful to Professor Ben Kimpel of Fort Smith, AR—co-biographer of Samuel Richardson, first novelist in English (*Pamela*)—for leading our small seminar, page by page, really, line by line, hand in hand through the dense woods of *The Cantos;* informally annotating whilst chain-smoking in his yolk-yellow shirt, interrupting his monologue only for a few seconds to rush to the slit of a corner window, worried that a sudden honking hail would be ruinous for his flower garden. So much for farm museums. (That was meant to be about farm museums.)

~

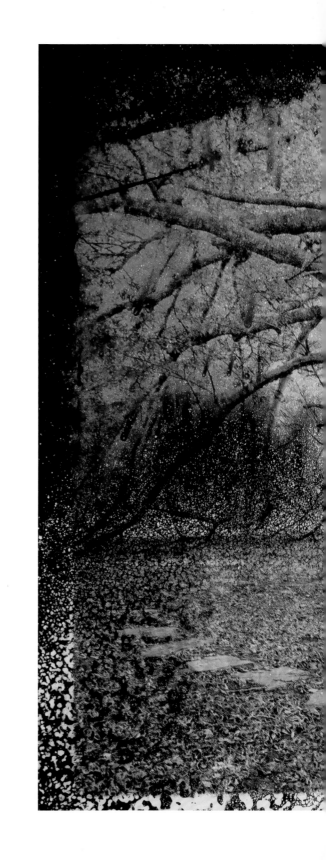

Mast has a short-range dispersal distance. There are researchers who conclude that when it happens it is often the work of the European jay, about 4,000 meters or 2½ miles; whereas by rodents, the distance tends to be under 100 meters.

Jays also bury seeds, helping them germinate. This supports the claim that these birds dispersed the fagaceous trees so quickly during the Holocene.

Seeds drop down plumb, so wind won't carry them far.

Others say the seeds are windblown.

Jays seem to pick out the good seeds. They can tell from the weight and the sound seeds make when they click on them with their beaks. And they eat only about a third of the ones they stash.

The jay can transport 14 beechnuts at a time. It is even conjectured that the jay beak was built for this exact transport.

Never plant a beech on level land.

Never plant a beech on soil with poor drainage.

Chalky and alkaline are its preferred soil types.

Salt-sensitive. Lime-tolerant.

The heartwood stores sugars, oils, dyes.

The heartwood is dead.

The heartwood holds up the tree.

The roots, ropelike. Hold the tent in place.

Beeches establish well at the edges of pine forests.

They have fine hairs on the underside and along the edge. These they lose.

Glabrous underleaf: no hair, no fur.

~

It is recommended that you plant a beech for the benefit of at least a couple of generations after you're gone.

The national register of Champion Trees was initiated in 1940. Evidently only 3 from that listing are, as they say, still with us.

~

Native in the human world is defined as pre-European contact. In anthropology, European contact with the native population has been designated the *shatter zone.*

~

Now the salt cedars (tamarisks) in Arizona have made themselves so unwelcome the tamarisk beetle is being encouraged to take them out. The tamarisks, like most living things in Arizona, are thirsty, and are considered to threaten the water supply. This may be true. Lake Mead, the Colorado's reservoir, is at its lowest since its filling in 1938. However, encouraging a leaf-eater… there will be consequences.

~

O rare! A postcard! from a poet of a beech at Fontainebleau. Photograph by Jean-Baptiste Gustave Le Gray, ca. 1857. The tree improbably suspended above its roost of roots. The luxuriant canopy, age-defiant. The print was sold by Sotheby's in 1999 for £419,500 to Sheikh Saud Al Thani of Qatar (in case you wondered where all the cool rare stuff was going these days).

To painters the beech has long been irresistible. A special appreciation to a few: English watercolorist Paul Sandby (1731–1809), Hudson River school painter Ashur Durand (1796–1886), Dutch artist Maria Philippina Bilders–van Bosse (1837–1900). Bilders-van Bosse exhibited at the 1893 Chicago World's Fair Expo. Bavarian-born Carl Christian Brenner (1838–1888), a tonalist, who immigrated to the US and often painted in Cherokee Park in Louisville. The tornado of 1974 destroyed many of the park's mature trees, including two groves of beeches. Vienna's gold-brushed Gustav Klimt (1862–1918); Englishmen Arthur Rackham (1867–1939), illustrator of J.M. Barrie's *Peter Pan in Kensington Gardens,* and E.H. Shepard (1879–1976), *Punch* political cartoonist best known, to his lasting regret, as the man who drew Pooh. English surrealist and war artist Paul Nash (1899–1946), who referred to the local beech groves as "the pyramids of [his] small world." German landscape artist Christian Ernst Bernhard Morgenstern (1805–1867), grandfather of poet Christian Morgenstern (1871–1914), whose beautiful silent poem "Fisches Nachtgesang" crops up, an old *Buchzeichen* in my head:

Fish's Nightsong:

May last, Belmont, MA, in front of the Belmont Women's Club, the former William Flagg Homer House: after more than 200 years the copper beeches have been cut. The trees are in the background of Winslow Homer's *The Croquet Game,* 1866. Three bonneted women in hoop-skirted, cinched dresses, one in red and white and one in blue and white, one in brown, black, and white. The woman in red is about to send a ball up-country. A man is positioning the ball. The woman in blue is either preparing for the send-off or suffering a mild headache from the sun or holding her brim against the breeze. The leafed-out trees fill the background. The Civil War is underway. Homer is illustrating for *Harper's*. He finagles his way to the front in Virginia. The leisure class is in an advanced stage of the game, *paille maille,* a French peasant's game brought to the US by the Irish. Strange otherworld. But it is inside this one, just as Éluard said.

Once David Hockney returned from Los Angeles to his native England, he painted *Bigger Trees Near Warter*. Finished in 2007, the series is composed of 50 canvases.

The photographers were quick to be on the scene. In the nascence of the art they were out with their hulky gear photographing beech trees already quite senior: Le Gray (*Beech Tree,* Fontainebleau, ca. 1857), Eugène Atget (*Villeneuve-l'Étang,* ca. 1910–1914), William Henry Fox Talbot (*Beech Trees at Lacock Abbey,* 1844), Vernon Heath (*Burnham Beeches,* 1871), also photographed the marriage of Prince of Wales and Victoria's Golden Jubilee garden party. James Sinclair, 14th Earl of Caithness, a beech then estimated to be 450 years old (1864). Sinclair also tutored the Prince of Wales and invented an artificial leg. Albert Renger-Patzsch (*Red Beech at Forest Edge,* 1947). Barbara Bosworth, born in Novelty, Ohio, photographed national champion trees in 23 states (including the American beech, champion in her native state, 1990). Then there are Tony Howell's knockout 2011 photograph of beech tree roots and Mitch Epstein's *New York Arbor* collection (2014).

In Louisville, Kentucky, an early Olmsted design, Cherokee Park, has attracted photographers (of beeches) for years: Theodore Paul Eitel's wet plates, Andy Christ's winter beeches; Elsie Kittredge's initial tree (1922); dance photographer Barbara Brooks Morgan's portrait of the painter Charles Sheeler in front of his favorite beech (1945); a 2009 aerial shot of a beech downed in a January ice storm, running out the tape at 165 feet.

~

The Yosemite Rim Fire stood at 222,777 acres September 2, 2013 (in 1988, all of 800,000 acres burned). At the end of June, the Yarnell Hill Fire (AZ) killed 19 firefighters. Is this part of what we are to get used to, to roll out of bed for—surgical masks for bad-air days, nonpotable water, neighborhoods engulfed in flames, vast spills of crude oil, overfished waters, animal extinctions, and contaminated soil:

fire *paper* *ash* *earth*

~

Movement needs to be figured into the equation. Not much stays put. More and more, *native* means the wiped-out population.

The 2,000 cherry trees gifted by Japan to Washington, DC, in 1910 were infested, and it was a touchy thing to let the Japanese know they had to be destroyed. About a dozen of the buggiest were spared for a scientist with:

a net *a cyanide bottle* *and lantern* *to watch over* *and study*

Graciously the Japanese replaced the destroyed cherries with
3,000-plus more cherries that cleared quarantine.

~

In Kyoto, the *sakuramori,* cherry tree doctor, looks after the most famous of
these in Maruyama Park, the White Single Petal Higan Weeping Sakura.

Toemon Sano, a 16th-generation sakuramori, attributes sickness in the cherry
trees to groundwater pollution.

The grey-water days are ahead. The grey-water days are upon us.

Even the eucs cannot save you from ague, blindness, and insanity nor even from
irritation and suspicion.

~

The average age of a tree in NYC is under 40 (about the span of an Aztec's life).

~

The apple tree never asks the beech how he shall grow, nor the lion the horse
how he shall take his prey.   William Blake

~

We are just back from the West and I am ready to see all the naked trees scratching the sky. New Year's Day, lobster-cold, time for a drive. Westerly is at the southern end of the state, 40-something miles. Once you adjust to Lil Rhody scale, you've become one of us, anything farther than the airport seems a fearsome autonomous region.

Civilized Westerly has a Victorian park in the middle of town, Wilcox Park, with a *Fagus sylvatica* dedicated to the 1952–1956 heavyweight champion Rocky Marciano, a nonnative of the state, but Italian (close enough to qualify). A rubber tree pays tribute to Ellison "Tarzan" Brown, a Narragansett Indian born in nearby Charlestown: won two Boston Marathons, once ran two marathons in one 24-hour trot, and was on the 1936 Olympic team. Born to run. Why a rubber tree I couldn't tell you, and we found neither Rocky's nor Tarzan's memorial trees. (Nor could I locate Maria Callas's niche in Père Lachaise. Twenty years on, I learned her ashes had long been removed from the cemetery and strewn in the Aegean.)

I saw my first purple fountain beech in Westerly and the toppled remains of a diseased beech felled last month by arborists-in-training. The stool would seat seven or eleven easy. (The record shows it was planted in 1898.) There were still many fine coppers and *F. sylvatica*. Also a sourwood that has a time capsule planted under its feet, to be opened a few short years from now. The sourwood is a bit of a froufrou act. Lord knows what they buried under its skirt. Bordering Westerly, exclusive Watch Hill, where 24-year-old country-now-pop sensation Taylor Swift plunked down $17.75 million (wire transfer) for a seaside vacation house and then built an enormous "eyesore" of a seawall affronting exclusive neighbors. And after a summer break-in, had a fence constructed plus hired a "crack-security team." Harkness House was originally built for a Standard Oil heiress. (It is a contrary pastime of mine to follow the money. For analysis see: Thomas Piketty.)

The park was designed by Warren H. Manning, another onetime associate of the ubiquitous Frederick Law Olmsted.

~

Come Monday, then come Wednesday when this polar vortex is predicted to withdraw, I will drive to Newport to watch one of Salve Regina's grandegrannydames come down, and another at a residence in the Bellevue district.

To others I say I am visiting these individuals (which doesn't mean I carry on a delusional dialogue with them like poor Richard Nixon wandering the White House halls talking to the portraits). It means I go to pay my respects, and discreetly to ogle. My approach is close to ceremonial—split-open ribcage, palpitating heart in hand.

~

True, I sappily envisioned an evening with old friends under hovering lanterns, among these sensational sessile beings, branches limbing low, flirty laughter, prosecco, whitefish and silver queen corn, blackberries, and enough caffeine and dark chocolate to steer one and all home without incident. I waken repeatedly to gnarly misgivings and adversarial imaginings—with developers, apparatchiks, celebrities, lobbyists, an endless cavalcade of the Nouveau Gilded Agers—in flaming dread of *us,* the next annihilating asteroid.

On a recent flight returning to California from DC, I asked the young man seated next to me, a Malek's Tree Service patch on his khaki shirt pocket, studying a book with a man on the cover straddling the branches of a eucalyptus, What made you decide to get into tree work. Let's see, he said, I thought to myself, I like nature, I like to climb things, and I love power tools.

> *water*   *minerals*   *air*   *light*

On the last day of the world / I would want to plant a tree   W.S. Merwin

~

ROOT HAIRS

(This list is only partial and has multiple sources named in the bibliography. Nor does the list promise to top off in the near future, providing the beech tree continues to reside among us.)

F. crenata, the Japanese beech, is sometimes called *F. sieboldii* for the German doctor who identified it near the Dutch East India Co.'s Deshima trading post in Japan, at 4,921 feet. A fine pic of a specimen at North Carolina State University's A&T Extension.

F. engleriana, Chinese beech (introduced to Arnold Arboretum, 1907).

F. grandifolia, only one of its kind: native to eastern North America, from Ontario to Nova Scotia, as far south as Texas and Florida.

F. sylvatica 'Albovariegata', a bud sport (part of the plant differs from the rest but remains in future propagations); leaves white streaked in a chimera, a single organism, has two genetically different kinds of tissue.

F. sylvatica 'Ansorgei', shrubby; introduced by Carl Ansorge, Hamburg, 1884. Rare in Europe, rarer yet in the US. More shrub than tree. A dwarf. Grafted onto American root stock. The 'Ansorgei' or thread-leaf looks more like a Japanese maple than a beech.

F. sylvatica 'Aurea Pendula', golden weeping beech, a pillar of gold (Holland, 1900), a bud sport or chimera of a weeping beech.

F. sylvatica 'Cochleata', undulate, snail-leaf beech, shrubby, slow growing (1840).

F. sylvatica 'Cristata', cockscomb beech (one in Wellesley, MA), described as the least attractive European beech in a 1938 issue of *Arnoldia* (from Arnold Arboretum).

F. sylvatica 'Cuprea', copper (1680, Buch, near Zurich).

F. sylvatica 'Dawyck', fastigiated, columnar (Scotland, 1860); 'Dawyck Gold'; 'Dawyck Purple'.

F. sylvatica 'Fastigiata', beech var. 'Dawyckii', all the branches erect. The original tree goes straight up. Fast. Like the Lombardy poplar. (There's a fine one at Arnold Arboretum.)

F. sylvatica var. *heterophylla* 'Asplenifolia', fern leaf (probably French in origin, 1804). There are fine specimens in Newport, RI. In England, it is recorded to have been in cultivation for a century. 'Asplenifolia' is hard to differentiate from *F. sylvatica* var. *heterophylla* 'Laciniata', cut-leaf (branch sport, Bohemia, 1792).

F. sylvatica f. latifolia, "the larger (to 4" × 6") green leaves of this stately large tree each have 7 to 9 'large bites' out of their edges... a handsome tree!" (Forestfarm nursery, Pacifica, OR).

F. sylvatica 'Mercedes', the dwarf of dwarves.

F. sylvatica 'Miltonensis', variant of 'Pendula' (is thought by some to be more beautiful than the 'Pendula' because its branches spread farther out before weeping. The original is in Milton Park, Northamptonshire, UK (1837). They are grown at Forestfarm and Stanley & Sons, Boring, OR.

F. sylvatica 'Pendula', weeping mushroom and fountain forms (England 1836), found in the wild in the forest of Brotonne, in Seine-Inférieure (now Seine-Maritime), France.

F. sylvatica 'Purpurea', purple beech (Germany, 1865). The first recorded instance of the purple beech growing in 3 or 4 places in central Europe published in 1680.

F. sylvatica 'Purpurea Pendula', narrow and slow growing. I saw one in Toronto creating a sliver of quivering shade.

F. sylvatica 'Quercifolia', oak-leaf beech.

F. sylvatica 'Riversii', purple beech, along with 'Spaethiana' and 'Swat Magret', darker than coppers. 'Riversii', 'Rohanii', 'Spaethiana' are the most common of standard *F. sylvatica* with purple leaves, often a copper beech. That's too many names of trees with too many similarities. The 'Riversii', or Rivers' Purple, is the most popular. Thomas Rivers & Sons, British nurserymen and pomologists, specialized in fruit trees and roses and Rivers' Purple beech. Thomas Rivers III is likely the one responsible for Rivers' Purple. Out of the original 300 acres, 5 remained under voluntary stewardship after the last parcel was sold by the family to developers in the 1980s. That stewardship ended in 2009. I don't know the rest of the story.

F. sylvatica 'Roseomarginata' (tricolor, France). There's one in Petaluma!

F. sylvatica 'Tortuosa', self-explanatory (France, Germany, Denmark, Sweden, 1825). Also called "parasol beech." Of French origin; it is found in the forest of Verzy, near Rheims. There's one at the Arnold. My assistant, Rowan Sharp, stood while I took her picture. Grinning in her winter coat. The tree going through its contortions behind her.

Louis the Plant Geek of Hopkinton, RI, calls the European beeches the Heinz pickles of trees (meaning, if you blink, there's a new cultivar). The more there are, the less beechy.

The W.J. Bean encyclopedia, *Trees and Shrubs Hardy in the British Isles,* 1970–76, lists 23 clones.

~

ACKNOWLEDGMENTS

Special gratitude to Chris Fletcher, arborist, Bartlett Tree Experts and Juniper Hill Cemetery, Bristol, for generously sharing his professional experience, extensive knowledge, and lyric relationship to trees, as well as his workshop and tours of outstanding beech trees in Newport, RI. And to Rowan Sharp, who assisted and accompanied for a semester on this amble. She was curious, effervescent, spot on.

Additional thanks to the inaugural Brown University Presidential Faculty Award (Christina H. Paxson, President), which provided funding and encouragement for this research. Thanks also to Dean Kevin McLaughlin at Brown University for his friendship and for his support and advocacy of C.D. Wright's work. Gratitude to Lisa Pearson, Head of Arnold Arboretum Horticultural Library and Archives, and to botanist Shelley Weisberg of the North Cascades Institute.

Copper Canyon Press also wishes to thank the anonymous donor whose support made this special edition possible.

~

Cliff, Jimmy. "The Harder They Come." *The Harder They Come*. Island Records, 1976.

Books and other printed sources: Bailey, L.H. *The Standard Cyclopedia of Horticulture*. New York: Macmillan, 1914–17; Berry, Edward Wilber. *Tree Ancestors: A Glimpse into the Past*. Baltimore: Williams & Wilkins, 1923; Blake, William. *The Marriage of Heaven and Hell*. London: Camden Hotten, 1868; Brown, John P., C.E. *Practical Arboriculture: How Forests Influence Climate, Control the Winds, Prevent Floods, Sustain National Prosperity: A Textbook for Railway Engineers, Manufacturers, Lumbermen, and Farmers*. Connersville, IN: Hennebery, 1906; Bunch, William R. *Street Trees in Southern New England*. T.P. Husband, J.M. Lawrence III, and A.R. Knight eds. Division of Forest Environment, Rhode Island Department of Environmental Management and

Cooperative Extension, University of Rhode Island, 1979; Carlsen, Spike. *A Splintered History of Wood*. New York: HarperCollins, 2008; Champlin, Richard L. *Trees of Newport on the Estates of the Preservation Society of Newport Co.* Carlisle, MA: Applewood, 1976; Cohu, Will. *Out of the Woods: The Armchair Guide to Trees*. London: Short Books, 2015; Dirr, Michael. *Manual of Woody Plants*. Champaign, IL: Stipes Publishing, 1990; Dunn, Robert. *Every Living Thing: Man's Obsessive Quest to Catalog Life, from Nanobacteria to New Monkeys*. New York: Harper Perennial, 2010; Epstein, Mitch. *New York Arbor*. Göttingen, Germany: Steidl, 2013; Evelyn, John. *Silva: or A Discourse of Forest Trees and the Propagation of Timber in His Majesty's Dominions, as It Was Delivered in the Royal Society, on the 15th of October 1662*. London: H. Colburn, 1825; Fennell, Aubrey, Carsten Krieger, and Kevin Hutchinson. *Heritage Trees of Ireland*. Cork: The Collins Press, 2014; Flagg, Wilson. *The Woods and By-Ways of New England*. Boston: James R. Osgood & Co., 1872; Gilfillan, Merrill. "Still Life with Beeches." *Small Weathers*. Jamestown, RI: Qua Books, 2004; Gillman, Jeff. *How Trees Die: The Past, Present, and Future of Our Forests*. Chicago: Westholme, 2015; Goethe, Johann Wolfgang von, and C.F. MacIntyre. *Goethe's Faust, Part 1: New American Version*. New York: New Directions, 1957; Gotthelf, Jeremias, trans. Susan Bernofsky. *The Black Spider*. New York: NYRB Classics, 2013; Gray, Robert. *The Tree*. New York: Simon & Schuster, 1993; Gray, Thomas. *Elegy Written in a Country Churchyard*. London: Robert Dodsley, 1751; Hageneder, Fred. *The Meaning of Trees: Botany, History, Healing, Lore*. San Francisco: Chronicle, 2005; Hayman, Richard. *Trees: Woodlands and Western Civilization*. London: Bloomsbury, 2004; Heath, Francis George. *Burnham Beeches*. London: Sampson Low, Marston, Searle, and Rivington, 1879; ———. *Sylvan Winter*. London: Kegan Paul Trench & Co., 1886; Hora, Bayard, consultant ed. *The Oxford Encyclopedia of Trees of the World*. Oxford: Oxford University Press, 1981; Hugo, Nancy Ross, and Robert Llewellyn. *Seeing Trees: Discover the Extraordinary Secrets of Everyday Trees*. Portland: Timber Press, 2011; Huntington, Annie Oakes. *Studies of Trees in Winter, a Description of the Deciduous Trees of Northeastern America*. Boston: Knight and Millet, 1901; Jacobson, Arthur Lee. *North American Landscape Trees*. Berkeley: Ten Speed Press, 1996; Jameson, W.C. *Buried Treasures of the Ozarks*. Atlanta: August House, 2006; Johnson, Hugh. *The World of Trees*. Oakland: University of California, 2010; Langley, Batty. *New Principles of Gardening*. London: Printed for A. Bettesworth and J. Batley, 1728; Little, Charles E. *The Dying of the Trees: The Pandemic in America's Forests*. New York: Penguin, 1997; Mabey, Richard. *Beechcombings:*

The Narratives of Trees. New York: Vintage, 2008; Maloof, Joan. *Teaching the Trees: Lessons from the Forest*. Athens, GA: University of Georgia, 2007; Martin, Robert Bernard. *Gerard Manley Hopkins: A Very Private Life*. London: Faber and Faber, 2011; Mathews, F. Schuyler. *Fieldbook of American Wildflowers*. New York: G.P. Putnam's Sons, 1909; Merwin, W.S. "Place." *The Rain in the Trees*. New York: Knopf, 1988; Nadkarni, Nalini M. *Between Earth and Sky: Our Intimate Connections to Trees*. Oakland: University of California, 2009; Pavord, Anna. *The Curious Gardener*. London: Bloomsbury, 2011; Peattie, Donald Culross. *A Natural History of North American Trees*. San Antonio: Trinity University, 2013; Perlin, John. *A Forest Journey: The Story of Wood and Civilization*. New York: Countryman Press, 2005; Russell, L.W. *Native Trees: A Study for School and Home*. Boston: New England Publishing Co., 1897; Russell, Tony, Catherine Cutler, and Martin Walters, eds. *The New Encyclopedia of American Trees*. London: Hermes House, 2009; Sargent, Charles Sprague. *Manual of the Trees of North America (Exclusive of Mexico)*. New York: Houghton Mifflin, 1922; Shakespeare, William. *As You Like It* (act 3, scene 2); Strutt, Jacob George. *Sylva Britannica: or, Portraits of Forest Trees*. London: Longman, Rees, Orme, Brown, and Green, 1830; Thomas, Graham S. *Trees in the Landscape*. New York: Saga, 2004; Thomas, Peter. *Trees: Their Natural History*. Cambridge: Cambridge University Press, 2000; Thoreau, Henry David. *The Journal of Henry David Thoreau*. New York: NYRB Classics, 2011; ———. *Walden; or, Life in the Woods*. Boston: Ticknor and Fields, 1854; Tudge, Colin. *The Tree: A Natural History of What Trees Are, How They Live, and Why They Matter*. New York: Broadway Books, 2006; Virgil. *Bucolics,* Ecologue (1.1–2); Weil, Simone. *The Need for Roots: Prelude to a Declaration of Duties Toward Mankind*. London: Routledge, 2001; Wessels, Tom. *Reading the Forested Landscape: A Natural History of New England*. New York: Countryman Press, 2005.

⁓

William Astifan, Director of Haverford Arboretum, Haverford College

Rachael Boast, poet (*Pilgrim's Flower,* Picador, 2013), UK, for telling me about her childhood experience

John T. Campanini, technical advisor, Rhode Island Tree Council, former City Forester, Providence, RI

Andrea Carneiro, Communications Manager, the Preservation Society of Newport County

Hope Coulter, teacher at Hendrix College, for contacting nurseryman Larry Lowman

Jeff Curtis, Director of Gardens and Grounds, Newport Preservation Society

Michael Dosmann, Keeper of the Living Collections, Arnold Arboretum, Boston, for generous conversation on beeches

Peter and Karen Graves, for hospitality of their beeches, Warwick Neck, RI

Donald Guravich, arborist, Bolinas, CA

George and Nannette Herrick, for hospitality of their beeches and Norwich terrier trio, on the day their favorite beech had to be taken down

Bill Hirst, Highland Hill Farm, Fountainville, PA, in conversation with Rowan Sharp, November 2012

James Holmberg, Curator, Historical Society, Louisville, KY

Arthur Lee Jacobson, Seattle, for his interview and walking tour with Rowan Sharp, December 2012

Dave Lindsay, Urbana, IL, in conversation with Rowan Sharp, November 2012 (re: all-day drive with his son to buy a copper beech from Highland Hills farm in Pennsylvania)

Larry Lowman, nurseryman, lifelong plantsman, and native plant expert, Carroll County, AR

Gabriel Malek, Malek's Tree Service, Santa Monica, CA

Fred Perry, Director of Horticulture, Blithewold Arboretum, Bristol, RI, walking tour of specimen trees

Kelly Perry, Chief Horticulturist at Swan Point Cemetery, Providence, RI

Mike Startup, horticulturist, Haverford Arboretum

Chad Uchtman, for the undue gift (in Little Rock) of *A Fieldbook of American Wildflowers,* a meticulous, pencil-annotated treasure he bought in a secondhand bookstore and thought to pass on

Kristyn A. Woodland, staff horticulturalist, Newport Tree Society, for the generous drive-around tour of Newport estate beeches

⁓

Blogs and other online sites: Allen, Gary. *On the Table: The Curious Home of Gary Allen* (blog). http://onthetable.us; Cameron, Peter. *Peter Cameron's Blog.* https://cameroncounts.wordpress.com; Clark, Curtiss. *The Field Notebook: Notes from the Natural World* (blog). http://www.field-notebook.com; Ernst, Crystal. "American Beech Tree (Fagus grandifolia)." *St. Lawrence Lowlands… natural history projects in the Morgan Arboretum.* October 29, 2012. https://stlawrencelowlands.wordpress.com; *(e) Science News.* http://esciencenews.com; Farlex. *The Free Library.* https://www.thefreelibrary.com; Gale Group. https://www.gale.com; GardenGuides.com; Gilleland, Michael. "Patulae Recubans Sub Tegmine Fagi." *Laudator Temporis Acti* (blog). March 9, 2008. http://laudatortemporisacti.blogspot.com; Keenan, Trevor. Nature.com. July 2013; Larson, Eric. GardenClips.com. March 12, 2012; Lattrell, Bill. *Wildramblings: Stories, Essays and Photos of a New England Ecologist* (blog). http://wildramblings.com; McEnnerney, Mike. "I Should Have Done This Years Ago!" *The Pedalling Photographer* (blog). November 21, 2013, https://thepedallingphotographer.com; *Newser.* June 11, 2011. http://www.newser.com; Pike, Sue. SeacoastOnline.com; Raymond, Louis. *Louis The Plant Geek* (blog). http://www.louistheplantgeek.com; Russell, James (blog) http://jamesrussellontheweb.blogspot.com; *Texas Escapes: A Magazine Written by Texans.* http://texasescapes.com; *Treeblog.* http://www.treeblog.co.uk; Wikipedia, https://www.wikipedia.org; *Wild Birds Unlimited.* https://www.wbu.com; Mystical World Wide Web (where the unexplained is explained).

Journals and periodicals (print and digital): *Arkansas Democrat-Gazette* (April 24, 2013); *Arnoldia,* quarterly magazine of Arnold Arboretum initiated as a bulletin by Charles Sprague Sargent, the arboretum's first director; Bell, Dan, arborist, Bell Horticulture. *Tree Views* (Annual Newsletter) 10, no. 1 (1996); Canham, Charles D., and P.L. Marks. *Canadian Journal of Forest Research* 33 (2003); *The Civic League Bulletin of Newport* 4 (July 1910); Denk, Thomas, and Guido W. Grimm. "The Biogeographic History of Beech Trees." *Elsevier: Review of Palaeobotany and Palynology* 158, no. 1 (December 2009); DeYoung, Don. "Space-Age Leaves." *Answers in Genesis* (August 19, 2012); Forester, Edward S. "Trees and Plants in Homer." *The Classical Review* 50 (July 1936); Forman, Benno. *American Seating Furniture 1630–1730: An Interpretive Catalogue.* Reviewed in *Winterthur Portfolio* 23, no. 4 (winter, 1988); *The Garden Magazine* 31 (April 1920); Gilman, Edward F., and Dennis G. Watson. "Fagus Sylvatica." *EDIS* (November 1993); *Green Horizons Newsletter* 11, no. 1 (winter 2007); *The Guardian* (March 26, 2009); Johnson, W. Carter, and Thompson Webb III. "The Role of Blue Jays (*Cyanocitta cristata L.*) in the Postglacial Dispersal of

Fagacious Trees in Eastern North America," *Journal of Biogeography* 16, no. 6 (1989); Johnston, Jack. *Science News* (January 15, 2009); McLaughlin, John. *Forest Research Note* (Ontario, November 13, 2012); McMurtrie, Cornelia Hanna. "The Beech in Boston." *Arnoldia* 42, no. 1 (winter 1982); *The Mining Journal* (March 1, 2009); *Nature Bulletin.* Forest Preserve District of Cook County (February 7, 2012); *The New York Times* (December 25, 2012 and January 5, 2014); Nilsson, Sven G. and Urban Wästljung. "Seed Predation and Cross-Pollination in Mast-Seeding Beech." *Ecology* 68, no. 2 (1987); *The Oregonian* (October 17, 2012); *The Post-Standard,* Syracuse, NY (July 21, 2002); *The Press Democrat,* Santa Rosa, CA (July 16, 2014); Reid, Eliza P. *Historical and Literary Botany* 1 (1826); Russell, L.W. "Native Forest Trees of Rhode Island, No. XVII." *Random Notes on Natural History* 3, no. 10 (October 1, 1886); Sheridan, Moira. Delawareonline; *Smithsonian Magazine* (January, 2013); Stocker, Carol. *The Boston Globe* (November 17, 2008); *Washington Post,* Health and Science (October 9, 2012); Wilson, Ernest H. (then Assistant Director of the Arnold Arboretum). "Bulletin of Popular Information." *Arnoldia* (June 1, 1927); ———. "The Romance of Our Trees—The Beeches." *The Garden Magazine* 31 (April 1920); White, Mel. "High in the Ozarks." *National Geographic* 214, no. 4, (October 2008); Wittig, Rüdiger, and Heinz Neite. "Acid Indicators Around the Trunk Base of Fagus Sylvatica in Limestone and Loess Beechwoods: Distribution Pattern and Phytosociological Problems." *Vegetatio* 64, no. 2/3 (January 1986).

Additional contributions to *Casting Deep Shade:*

Alfred Baker, farmer, planted copper beech, 1885, Troutdale, OR

Dan Bell, Rhode Island horticulturist

Peter Cameron, London mathematician, blue jay seed distribution

Charles Douglas, 6th Marquess of Queensberry

Robert W. Freckmann, lightning conduction and beech trees

B. Heinze and T.H. Gerburek, 1995 search for dominant gene linked to leaf color

Robert L. Heyd, Forest Health Specialist, Michigan Department of Natural Resources

Dr. George Hudler, plant pathologist, Cornell University

Olavi Huikari, beech tree DNA researcher

Rodney Johnson, carver of Cherokee syllabary on a gourd

Thomas Jung, independent scientist in Brannenburg, Germany

Pehr Kalm, 18th-century Finnish-Swedish botanist

Alan Kaplan naturalist, Tilden Nature Area, Berkeley, CA

Edwin H. Ketchledge, dubbed the Adirondacks "the infection court"

Gerd Krüssman, Director, Dortmann Botanical Gardens, 1950

Robert Linderman, research plant pathologist for USDA Agricultural Research Service

Hermann Merkel, Chief Forester, Bronx Zoo, discovered blight on chestnut trees in 1904

R. Robinson and H. Smith, 1955, anthocyanin pigments research

Charles Sprague Sargent, Arnold Arboretum's first director

David Sears, early Brookline, MA, developer

Ellie Siegel, writer

Michael Snyder, commissioner of Vermont Forests, Parks, and Recreation

Douglas Stahlman (1861–1942), carver of the Bible Tree

James Stidfole, wood artist, Eugene O'Neill Theater

Rachel Sussman, Smithsonian photographer of trees 2,000 years or older

Peter Thomas, observed beech tree resistance to sulfur dioxide

Harvey Updyke Jr., poisoner of oaks in Auburn, AL

William Warren, cognitive scientist, Rhode Island

Jim and Ann Wilderom, Harbor Springs, MI

Ernest H. Wilson, plant explorer and director (after Sargent), Arnold Arboretum, 1920s

Phil Zamora, lead singer, Cream tribute band

PS: Donations in Essie Burnworth's name can be made to the Maryland chapter of the American Chestnut Foundation.

PPS: Wild Pantry, P.O. Box 67, Coker Creek, TN 37314, sometimes carries beechnuts (Gary Allen, "Food Writer and Dilettante").

PPSs: "Little Fucker[s]" is a Vic Chesnutt song recorded on *Dark Developments* with Elf Power and the Amorphous Strums.

"Taken in all seasons and judged by all that makes a tree noble—strength combined with grace, balance, longevity, hardiness, health—the Beech is all that we want a tree to be."   Donald Culross Peattie

And more.

LIST OF ILLUSTRATIONS

pp. 143–49 *Beech Tree Roots #51; Beech Tree #26; Beech Tree #4 (Warren); Beech Tree Roots #37.* Photographic monoprints by Denny Moers, 2015–18.

p. 158 Bluebells under a beech. Photograph by the author.

p. 159 C.D. Wright at Robert Creeley's gravesite, Mount Auburn Cemetery, Cambridge, MA, 2014. Photograph by Denny Moers.

p. 161 Daniel Boone tree. Filson Historical Society, Louisville, Kentucky.

p. 168 RHi X17 3659, Downed tree, Providence, RI, September 1938. Silver gelatin print. Courtesy the Rhode Island Historical Society.

p. 169 RHi X17 3656, Downed tree across road; RHi X1 3657, Downed tree on lawn; RHi X17 3658, Downed tree. Providence, RI, September 1938. Silver gelatin prints. Courtesy the Rhode Island Historical Society.

p. 177 *Burnham Beeches.* English engraving, 1882. Artokoloro Quint Lox Limited/Alamy.

pp. 183–89 *Beech Tree #9; Beech Tree Roots #38; Beech Tree #48; Beech Tree #45.* Photographic monoprints by Denny Moers, 2015–18.

p. 196 Miura folds. Drawing by Phil Kovacevich.

p. 197 Photograph by Jessica M. Winder (https://natureinfocus.blog).

p. 201 Leaning beech trees. Source unknown.

p. 205 Kerner, J. (1783). *Beschreibung und Abbildung der Bäume und gesträuche, welche in dem herzogthum Wirtemberg wild wachsen.* Stuttgart: Christoph Friedrich Cotta. Arnold Arboretum Horticultural Library Collection.

p. 221 Brunnenberg Castle, home of Ezra Pound's daughter, Mary de Rachewiltz.

pp. 223–29 *Beech Tree #31 (Creeley's Tree, Mt. Auburn Cemetery); Beech Tree #1; Beech Tree #66,* print 'A'; *Beech Tree #60,* print 'A'. Photographic monoprints by Denny Moers, 2015–18.

p. 236 *Bigger Trees Nearer Warter, Winter 2008.* Painting by David Hockney, oil on nine canvases. Photograph by Richard Schmidt.

p. 247 Rowan Sharp at the Arnold Arboretum. Photograph by the author.

p. 259 C.D. Wright, Eureka Springs, AK, January 6, 1983. Photograph by Forrest Gander.

ABOUT THE AUTHOR

C.D. Wright grew up in Arkansas. She was the author of more than a dozen collections of poetry and prose and a recipient of numerous awards, including a MacArthur Fellowship. *One With Others: a little book of her days* won the National Book Critics Circle Award and the Lenore Marshall Prize and was a finalist for the National Book Award. Her book *Rising, Falling, Hovering* won the 2009 International Griffin Poetry Prize. Wright was married to writer/translator Forrest Gander and taught at Brown University. She unexpectedly passed away in her sleep on January 12, 2016.

Poetry is vital to language and living. Since 1972, Copper Canyon Press has published extraordinary poetry from around the world to engage the imaginations and intellects of readers, writers, booksellers, librarians, teachers, students, and donors.

WE ARE GRATEFUL FOR THE MAJOR SUPPORT PROVIDED BY:

 THE PAUL G. ALLEN FAMILY FOUNDATION

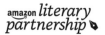 amazon *literary partnership*

 the POint *envision·enact·evolve*

 4 CULTURE

 golden lasso

Lannan

 ART WORKS. National Endowment for the Arts arts.gov

 A& OFFICE OF ARTS & CULTURE SEATTLE

 WASHINGTON STATE ARTS COMMISSION

Anonymous

Jill Baker and Jeffrey Bishop

Anne and Geoff Barker

Donna and Matt Bellew

John Branch

Diana Broze

Sarah and Tim Cavanaugh

Beatrice R. and Joseph A. Coleman Foundation

Laurie and Oskar Eustis

Mimi Gardner Gates

Linda Gerrard and Walter Parsons

Nancy Gifford

Gull Industries Inc. on behalf of Ruth and William True

The Trust of Warren A. Gummow

Phil Kovacevich and Eric Wechsler

Lakeside Industries Inc. on behalf of Jeanne Marie Lee

Maureen Lee and Mark Busto

Rhoady Lee and Alan Gartenhaus

Ellie Mathews and Carl Youngmann as The North Press

Anne O'Donnell and John Phillips

Petunia Charitable Fund and adviser Elizabeth Hebert

Gay Phinney

Suzie Rapp and Mark Hamilton

Emily and Dan Raymond

Jill and Bill Ruckelshaus

Kim and Jeff Seely

Richard Swank

University Research Council of DePaul University

Vincentian Endowment Foundation

Dan Waggoner

Barbara and Charles Wright

Caleb Young and Keep It Cinematic

The dedicated interns and faithful volunteers of Copper Canyon Press

TO LEARN MORE ABOUT UNDERWRITING COPPER CANYON PRESS TITLES, PLEASE CALL 360-385-4925 EXT. 103

Lannan Literary Selections

For two decades Lannan Foundation has supported the publication and distribution of exceptional literary works. Copper Canyon Press gratefully acknowledges their support.

LANNAN LITERARY SELECTIONS 2018

Sherwin Bitsui, *Dissolve*

Jenny George, *The Dream of Reason*

Ha Jin, *A Distant Center*

Aimee Nezhukumatathil, *Oceanic*

C.D. Wright, *Casting Deep Shade*

RECENT LANNAN LITERARY SELECTIONS FROM COPPER CANYON PRESS

Josh Bell, *Alamo Theory*

Marianne Boruch, *Cadaver, Speak*

Olena Kalytiak Davis, *The Poem She Didn't Write and Other Poems*

Michael Dickman, *Green Migraine*

John Freeman, *Maps*

Deborah Landau, *The Uses of the Body*

Maurice Manning, *One Man's Dark*

Rachel McKibbens, *blud*

W.S. Merwin, *The Lice*

Camille Rankine, *Incorrect Merciful Impulses*

Roger Reeves, *King Me*

Paisley Rekdal, *Imaginary Vessels*

Brenda Shaughnessy, *So Much Synth*

Richard Siken, *War of the Foxes*

Frank Stanford, *What About This: Collected Poems of Frank Stanford*

Ocean Vuong, *Night Sky with Exit Wounds*

Javier Zamora, *Unaccompanied*

Ghassan Zaqtan (translated by Fady Joudah), *The Silence That Remains*

Cover art: Denny Moers, *Beech Tree #1* (detail), 2015–18.
Designed by Phil Kovacevich

Copper Canyon Press is in residence at Fort Worden State Park
in Port Townsend, Washington, under the auspices of Centrum.
Centrum is a gathering place for artists and creative thinkers
from around the world, students of all ages and backgrounds,
and audiences seeking extraordinary cultural enrichment.

LIBRARY OF CONGRESS CATALOGING-IN-PUBLICATION DATA
Names: Wright, C. D., 1949-2016, author.
Title: Casting deep shade : an amble inscribed to beech trees & co. / C.D. Wright.
Description: Port Townsend, Washington : Copper Canyon Press, [2019] |
Includes bibliographical references.
Identifiers: LCCN 2018032580 | ISBN 9781556595486 (hardcover : alk. paper)
Subjects: LCSH: Beech--Miscellanea.
Classification: LCC PS3573.R497 A6 2019 | DDC 813/.54—dc23
LC record available at https://lccn.loc.gov/2018032580

LIBRARY OF CONGRESS CONTROL NUMBER 2018032580

9 8 7 6 5 4 3 2 FIRST PRINTING

Copper Canyon Press
Post Office Box 271
Port Townsend, Washington 98368

www.coppercanyonpress.org